NOLS
SOFT PATHS

Third edition

NOLS
SOFT PATHS

How to Enjoy the Wilderness without Harming It

Third Edition

Bruce Hampton and David Cole

Illustrations by Denise Casey

STACKPOLE
BOOKS

Published by
STACKPOLE BOOKS
5067 Ritter Road
Mechanicsburg, PA 17055
www.stackpolebooks.com

Printed in the United States of America

10 9 8 7 6 5 4 3 2 1

Third edition

Cover design by Caroline Stover
Cover photograph by Deborah Sussex

Information for the graphs used in chapter 11 is adapted from *Bear Attacks* by Stephen Herrero by permission of The Lyons Press.

Quotations by Barry Lopez excerpted from *Arctic Dreams*.
Copyright © 1986 by Barry Holstun Lopez.
Reprinted with the permission of Charles Scribner's Sons.

Library of Congress Cataloging-in-Publication Data

Hampton, Bruce.
    NOLS soft paths : how to enjoy the wilderness without harming it / Bruce Hampton and David Cole.— 3rd ed.
        p. cm.
    Revised ed. of: Soft path. 2nd ed. 1995.
    Includes bibliographical references and index.
    ISBN 0-8117-2691-6
    1. Outdoor recreation—Environmental aspects—United States.
2. Wilderness areas—Environmental aspects—United States. I. Title: National Outdoor Leadership School soft paths. II. Cole, David. III. Hampton, Bruce. Soft path. IV. National Outdoor Leadership School (U.S.) V. Title.
GV191.4 .H36 2003
333.78—dc21   2002153633

Contents

Foreword

When I read *Soft Paths* in 1995, I was working in the outdoor recreation field for the first time. Though I grew up in Colorado and had spent much of my time outside camping with my family and later running and hiking the foothills of the Rocky Mountains, much of the book's information was new to me. *Soft Paths* struck a chord with me immediately, but I thought, "How am I ever going to digest all of this Leave No Trace, minimum impact information?"

After seven years with the program, I have a changed attitude about Leave No Trace skills and ethics. Leave No Trace is not simply about remembering exactly what minimum impact skill you can practice in every outdoor situation—how far you should camp from water, where to pitch your tent, how to build a fire or if you should build one in the first place. Rather, it is first and foremost an attitude and an ethic. Leave No Trace is about respecting and caring for wild lands, doing your part to protect our limited resources and future recreation opportunities. Once this attitude is adopted and the outdoor ethic is sound, the specific skills and techniques become second nature.

Beyond a personal commitment, there are many practices and details to be learned in order to make the best possible decisions when enjoying the outdoors. *Soft Paths* is an excellent resource for both shaping an outdoor ethic and providing these details. The text is comprehensive and practical. It provides specific minimum impact ideas, skills, and techniques that allow people of many different experience levels to learn and understand their role in protecting wildlands. The text is user-friendly, allowing readers to enjoy the book from start to finish or skip around from chapter to chapter. You are in good hands: NOLS—as a founding partner and currently the leading educational partner of Leave No Trace, Inc.—has developed much of the Leave No Trace curriculum based primarily on the information contained in *Soft Paths*.

Perhaps the most important information provided here explains *why* Leave No Trace is so essential today. Many of the skills and techniques are based on research that specifically examines human recreational impacts. Many times people don't feel as though one small action or behavior can make a difference—positive or negative. I am committed to the idea that equipped with Leave No Trace skills and techniques, we can drastically reduce our recreational impacts and not only maintain but improve the condition of wild and natural lands, one person at a time.

Settle down with this book, get a sense of the ethic, learn the finer points. Then ask yourself, "What would my last outing say about me?" You will never "get outside" the same way again.

Dana Watts, Executive Director
Leave No Trace, Inc.

Larkspur

And what will be the disposition of the landscape? Will it be used, as always, in whatever way we will, or will it one day be accorded some dignity of its own?

—Barry Lopez, *Arctic Dreams*

About This Edition

When we first wrote *Soft Paths* in 1987, our goal was to expand awareness of camping and travel practices that minimize damage caused by outdoor recreationists in wildlands. Utilizing practical techniques developed for over two decades, we explained what individual recreationists could do to minimize their impact on wilderness and remote backcountry areas, thus preventing these pristine lands from being "loved to death."

Since that first edition, the need to enjoy wilderness without harming it has become increasingly profound. Wilderness use and impact continue to grow at an astonishing rate, making it more imperative than ever to walk on "soft paths."

About the time that *Soft Paths* appeared, many federal and state land managers were beginning to realize that public education was the key to minimizing human impacts on wildlands. In the early 1990s, the United States Forest Service (USFS) led the way with a national wilderness ethics program called Leave No Trace.

From the start, NOLS has been intimately involved with Leave No Trace, helping bring together the four major land management agencies—the U.S. Forest Service, Bureau of Land Management, National Park Service,

Western   *Hemlock*

and U.S. Fish and Wildlife Service—with manufacturers, outdoor retailers, user groups, educators, and individuals who share a commitment to maintain and protect our wildlands and natural areas for future enjoyment.

In 1994, Leave No Trace, Inc., was spun off as its own non-profit organization, located in Boulder, Colorado. Today, it has grown into a national program that brings its message to millions of outdoor recreationists. NOLS is proud to partner with Leave No Trace, Inc., providing materials, training, and curriculum for educators throughout the nation. Building on material originally presented in *Soft Paths*, NOLS, in conjunction with LNT, produces pamphlets, videos, and training courses to educate wildland user groups, federal land management agencies, and the public on the best minimum-impact techniques for a variety of environments, including alpine areas, coasts, deserts, rivers, and lakes.

Today, you may see Leave No Trace messages in magazines, on television, and on the packaging of sporting goods. Readers of *Soft Paths* will readily recognize close parallels between the practices in this book and those of the Leave No Trace program.

New research has been steadily conducted since the first edition was published. The results of this work help us prescribe better minimum-impact techniques for wilderness use. Many readers have asked us for expanded discussions of the rationale behind recommended camping practices. We have included this new research and provide more explanation without getting into too much technical detail.

Some of the recommended practices have been changed from previous editions on the basis of additional field experience, and we've incorporated Leave No Trace principles into the text. Statistics, graphs, and photos have been updated since the first

Great Grey Owl

edition, and the bibliography has been expanded and updated for those who want the latest additional sources of information.

It's clear that wild-country travelers want to invest in the future of the lands they love to explore. We're grateful for the interest and enthusiasm that the original *Soft Paths* and the Leave No Trace program have generated. Acknowledgment of the great value of the earth's remaining wilderness is growing; so too is the willingness to develop a new relationship with the lands that bring us all so much joy.

—Bruce Hampton and David Cole

Acknowledgments

No single person can take credit for the practical conservation skills developed in these pages. Rather, these techniques have evolved through constant refinement and improvement during the past forty years, thanks to the efforts of the best outdoor educators in the world. To past and present outdoor instructors we gratefully dedicate this book.

We owe special thanks to a growing number of reviewers and writers who have helped make each edition so successful, particularly Molly Absolon and Tom Reed. In this latest edition, Glenn Goodrich, John Gookin, Jeff Marion, Buck Tilton, and Dana Watts provided thoughtful insight and advice.

The fine drawings of wilderness plants and animals are the work of Denise Casey, a talented Wyoming artist. Thanks also go to the Teton Science School for use of the Murie Collection.

We're grateful to both the NOLS Board of Trustees and the Leave No Trace, Inc., Board for their encouragement and determination in keeping the advice and techniques found in these pages before the public eye. Finally, we owe lasting thanks to Paul Petzoldt, the founder of NOLS, who first taught us to care for wildlands and then showed us how to teach others.

We have met the enemy and he is us.

—"Pogo," by Walt Kelly

1

The Case for Minimum Impact

From the Appalachian Mountains in the eastern United States, to the deserts of Baja California, to the high peaks of California's Sierra Nevadas, and to the remote coastlines of Alaska, the story is the same: user impact is spreading faster than land managers can control it. People visit the backcountry because they both value and enjoy it, but in the words of one observer, "We are loving our wilderness to death." The following scenarios are typical:

- In the Pacific Northwest, some high lake basins are visited by up to twenty-five thousand people in a snow-free season of less than ten weeks.
- Popular campsites in the Boundary Waters Canoe Area of Minnesota have suffered an 80 percent loss of vegetation.
- So many hikers have traversed the Old Bridle Path up New Hampshire's Mount Lafayette that the trail has eroded into a gully four feet deep, prompting trail crews to call it the "Old Bridle Trench."

Recreational use of America's wildlands has exploded in the past forty years. Since passage of the 1964 Wilderness Act, wilderness recreational users have increased more than sixfold. Much of this increase occurred during the 1960s when backpacking first became popular, but use has continued to grow as our country's population has expanded. Today our wilderness lands host close to 20 million visitor-days per year (a twelve-hour stay by one person). Recent studies indicate that the number of Americans who backpack increased more than 70 percent between 1982 and 1994, and the number of Americans who hiked increased more than 90 percent. In National Park Service backcountry, where use statistics are most reliable, overnight visitation increased at an annual rate of about 10 percent throughout the 1990s.

As the number of backcountry visitors grows, our responsibility to the land changes. No longer is it enough to simply pick up litter and extinguish matches. These efforts help, but wilderness is more than just an unspoiled environment. We need to be concerned about two dimensions of recreational impact: damage to the integrity of the land and injury to the wilderness experience of others.

Solution by Default

In his book *Basic Rockcraft*, Royal Robbins says, "A simple equation exists between freedom and numbers: the more people, the less freedom." Today, this maxim guides many public land managers in their attempt to strike a balance between providing free and unconfined access to backcountry recreation, and protecting the wildland environment from these same recreationists.

In 1991, researchers Jeff Marion, Joe Roggenbuck, and Bob Manning asked National Park Service managers what they were doing to minimize impact problems in the backcountry. They found that more than half of all parks limited group size and length of stay, and required that overnight visitors have permits. In addition, approximately 40 percent restricted the total number of people allowed to enter the backcountry.

The lands managed by the Forest Service, the Bureau of Land Management, and the Fish and Wildlife Service have fewer restrictions on their use than national parks, but the trend at all agencies has been toward more regulation. One need not look far for examples. Managers of the Linville

BILL PETERSEN

Since 1965, recreational use of wilderness has grown nearly 600 percent, resulting in impact not only to the environment but to the wilderness experience as well.

Gorge Wilderness in North Carolina allow a maximum of thirty individuals per day to enter the area. In Yellowstone National Park, users must obtain a permit before hiking into the backcountry, and campsites are designated. Only seven parties per day are allowed to launch on Idaho's Middle Fork of the Salmon River.

Sometimes such restrictions are unavoidable. But often they come too late, after the damage is already done. No one who values wilderness wants to see these lands suffer more abuse. Yet is the only solution to tell users how to camp, where to camp, and how long to stay? Many of us, after all, seek the solitude and freedom of wildlands as temporary relief from a restrictive society.

The underlying premise of this book is a belief that most damage to wildlands is the result of lack of education, not malice. In fact, it would be difficult to find a more intelligent, more caring group of individuals; most backcountry users are anxious to do the right thing. Yet good intentions alone have fallen short.

The Path to a Wildland Ethic

Minimum-impact backcountry use is a hands-on, practical approach to caring about both the land and the people who share its richness. Its success hinges on the willingness of the individual user to learn, to think, and then to commit knowledge to action. The resulting techniques are flexible and tempered by judgment and experience. They depend more on attitude and awareness than on rules and regulations. As individuals and organizations, we must care enough about the land to be willing to change our techniques and attitudes about what is appropriate behavior in the outdoors.

"Rules are for fools," NOLS founder Paul Petzoldt used to say. But Petzoldt wasn't advocating anarchy. He was reminding users that the most successful approach to being light on the land is to use good judgment, not to follow a set of rules blindly.

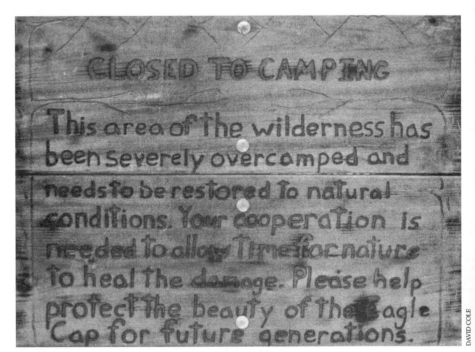

Restrictions most often come after the damage is already done.

The Leave No Trace program expresses the essence of minimum-impact camping in seven basic principles:

- Plan ahead and prepare.
- Travel and camp on durable surfaces.
- Dispose of waste properly.
- Leave what you find.
- Minimize campfire impacts.
- Respect wildlife.
- Be considerate of other visitors.

These principles are interwoven throughout the pages that follow and serve as guidelines that can be returned to time and again when trying to make ethical decisions about wildland use. The minimum-impact techniques described in this book are adaptable to changing conditions. Visitors must consider the variables of each backcountry decision—the soil, the vegetation, the wildlife, moisture, the amount and type of use the area receives, individual and group abilities, and the overall effect of their own use—and then use their judgment to determine which practices to apply.

We believe that an absolute, step-by-step Leave No Trace rule book can never and should never be written. We don't seek to dictate anyone's actions or ethics. We strive to tap users' obvious love of the backcountry and challenge them to use up-to-date and evolving minimum-impact techniques.

The practices outlined by the Leave No Trace principles demonstrate ways we can care for our wildlands, but more important, they point to a larger relationship that is the inevitable goal of any land ethic. Perhaps this relationship is best expressed in the beliefs of an old Eskimo man, related by the early twentieth-century arctic explorer Knud Rasmussen: "His philosophy of life was to the effect that we human beings know so very little of life and its controlling forces that we have an imperative duty, not only to ourselves but also to those we hold dear, to live as carefully as possible . . ."

By accepting responsibility for our remaining wildlands, we may take even better care of all of Earth's landscapes.

2

Backcountry Travel

Examine the gear of someone who is about to embark on a backcountry journey, and you are likely to find organized piles of lightweight equipment—everything from maps with trimmed borders to a toothbrush with a shortened handle. Why such fastidious organization? Because a successful trip depends on careful preparation and bringing just the right equipment.

These days, thoughtful backcountry visitors are asking another question: How can I travel through wildlands so that I make as little impact as possible? Many are learning that the same care and planning that contribute to a successful journey also serve to minimize disturbance to other visitors and the environment. If backcountry travelers find themselves wet and cold without the necessary equipment or clothes, they may be forced to build a large, environmentally destructive fire to stay warm. Visitor safety is clearly the priority, but careful planning often precludes unnecessary impact.

Methods of wildland travel vary greatly, but motorized recreation in federally designated wilderness is in most cases prohibited, making hiking, horseback riding, and boating the primary modes of transportation for most visitors. Although many of our recommendations apply to all methods, this chapter looks primarily at how to reduce the impact of the most frequent mode of backcountry travel: hiking. Later chapters deal with the specifics of travel with pack stock and boats.

The Impact of Hiking

A superficial look at the numbers raises doubts about whether there really is an impact problem caused by back-country travelers. Although wilderness areas are visited by millions each year, use intensity averages only about 0.2 visitor-days per acre annually. That's less than a single three-hour visit by one person—not much compared with other kinds of land use. Yet according to a 1980 survey of land managers conducted by researchers Randy Washburne and David Cole, crowding was a problem in *Columbine* more than half of all wilderness areas. Why are so many managers complaining of crowding if visitor use is so low?

Visitors don't distribute themselves evenly across our wildlands. Most use is concentrated in a few specific places in a few specific wilderness areas. In fact, more than half of all wilderness use occurs in a mere 10 percent of the total 100 million acres of designated wilderness. Similarly, in most wilderness areas, over half of all use occurs on only about 10 percent of the trail miles.

Visitation is also unevenly distributed over the course of the year. Certain seasons tend to be popular; others see little use. Weekend and holiday use is also high. In Yosemite National Park, for example, wilderness use on Memorial Day weekend is five times as great as on the weekends that follow. With this in mind, it is easy to see why crowding is a problem in many wilderness areas.

Examining why so few acres are favored is even more revealing. The popular spots are often close to population centers—areas with easy access, scenic views, or attractions such as good fishing or pleasant camping. Researchers have learned that within these areas, people generally prefer to go where others have traveled; most often this means following a trail.

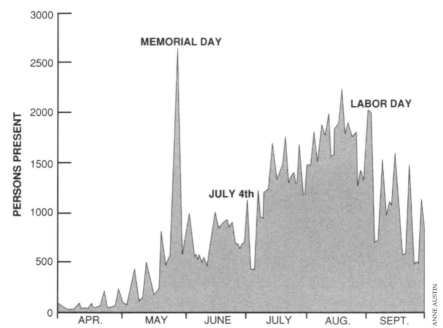

Weekend and holiday use is high in many backcountry destinations. In Yosemite National Park, for example, wilderness use on Memorial Day weekend is five times as great as on the weekends that follow.

The Trail Dilemma

Why do people concentrate on trails? Sometimes travel off established trails is prohibited or impractical, perhaps even dangerous; sometimes visitors just like the familiarity and ease of following constructed paths. Whatever the explanation, we users are profoundly affecting the areas we like the most. Trails may be a small part of the wilderness acreage, but they are crucial to our wilderness experience because we spend most of our time along them.

But trails are declining in number. In the 1930s, our national forests had 132,000 miles of trails; today there are fewer than 100,000 miles. The reasons for the decline are many. The primary one, however, is that land managers

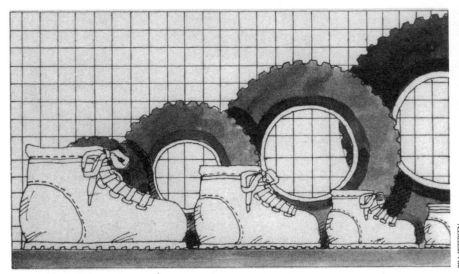

Road mileage in national forests has increased as trail miles have declined, yet trail use has grown fivefold since 1965.

deemphasized trails when fire control and timber harvesting became increasingly mechanized. As a result, road mileage increased while the number of trails declined. Today, although our national forest backcountry has 25 percent fewer trails, the public's use of trails has grown steadily. For every person hiking a trail in 1960, more than three people now leave their bootprints.

Increased trail use has prompted more than half of all wilderness managers to list human-caused soil erosion and injury to vegetation as major problems on trails. The next most widespread trail problem is erosion caused by horses, mules, burros, and other pack stock. Although only 11 percent of all parties entering the wilderness use pack animals, pack stock damage on or near trails is considered a problem in almost half our wilderness areas.

Today, new trails are mostly wishful thinking, and existing trail maintenance budgets have been cut back severely. Some land managers have recommended increased off-trail use in the belief that visitor impact will spread more evenly throughout the backcountry, resulting in less damage to established trails. But cross-country travel has proven no panacea, say its opponents; indeed, the worst nightmare for these managers is a backcountry that looks in its entirety like their most heavily eroded trail. They point to how thought-less off-trail use in New Hampshire's White Mountains resulted in having to limit travel strictly to trails. By 1977, surrounding alpine vegetation had suffered so much from cross-country use that scree walls were needed on both sides of a path to keep hikers confined to the trail.

As a user, you're often faced with a choice: Should you travel off-trail or on-trail? Our answer is that depending on local regulations, your evaluation of the land, and your skill in minimum-impact techniques, either choice can be appro-priate. Although heavy use of existing trails does increase contact with other visitors, staying on them is a good way to avoid disturbing fragile areas. When trails are well designed and maintained, they can accommodate a great deal of use and minimize impact—particularly in popular areas.

There are times, however, when cross-country travel is appropriate. Highly skilled travelers can often minimize their impact by choosing an off-trail route, but they have to be willing to exert special care. The message is clear: The user must carefully consider the trade-offs when deciding whether to travel by trail or cross-country.

Traveling on Trails
Even traditional, well-established trails can suffer abuse. Problems surface when they receive too much traffic or when hikers walk out of the established tread. Properly designed and maintained trails rarely suffer if visitors simply stay on them. But not all trails are well designed or properly main-tained. What happens when they deteriorate, and how can we minimize the damage?

The major environmental problems with trails are ero-sion, muddy stretches, and the development of informal

When horseback riders and sometimes hikers don't stay within the confines of a trail, multiple trails result (left). Hiking on the outside of a muddy trail breaks down the edge and widens the path. At right, the first and last hikers demonstrate the correct method.

trails. Most often, the solutions to erosion and muddiness are effective trail location, engineering, and maintenance. These are the responsibilities of the wilderness manager. Still, there are several things visitors can do to avoid contributing to further damage.

When following existing trails, walk single file and stay on the path. This is an important part of concentrating impact. Walking outside the tread—for example, traveling abreast or trying to avoid rocks or mud—breaks down the trail edge and widens the path. Such behavior also leads to the development of multiple trails, which scar some of our most beautiful meadows. Staying on trails is sometimes difficult when conditions are wet, yet this is when they are the most susceptible. Wearing a pair of well-fitted gaiters allows the hiker to walk briefly through wet or muddy areas while remaining dry.

As with muddy stretches, it's better to cross low-angled snowbanks than to skirt them and thus create additional trails. If you're familiar with the area and know where the trail is under the snow, tramp a path to lead the way for others. When crossing high-angled snowbanks, however, safety is often the foremost concern; in this case, there may be no alternative to skirting the snowbank. Here it's better to risk widening the path by walking on the edge of the trail than to encourage the development of an entirely new impromptu trail. Sometimes merely avoiding popular backcountry areas during wet periods such as the spring thaw is the best practice.

To limit erosion, trails are typically designed in such a way that steep grades are avoided. Where trails negotiate steep hills, the grade is kept low by using switchbacks. Many hikers are tempted at times to shorten their distance by shortcutting these switchbacks. Yet by doing this, hikers cause erosion and damage to vegetation. If the slope is vegetated, the first shortcutters probably just damage a few plants. But if the plants die, their roots no longer bind the soil, and soon the topsoil begins to wash away. Without topsoil, other plants can't recolonize the site, and the shortcut becomes a barren trench. Runoff and erosion accelerate. Eventually the shortcut becomes impassable, stripping away the corner of the switchback. Once erosion begins, it's hard to stop, and it may become impossible for nature to repair itself, particularly at high altitudes where growth is slow. If you come upon shortcuts, you can help by throwing brush or logs across them to block hiker access. If an established switchback is impassable because of erosion or mud, walk on hard surfaces (such as rock, sand, or snow) as much as possible, and notify the managers responsible for that area. You may be surprised what action a few voices of concern can bring.

Shortcutting trail switchbacks accelerates erosion, resulting in a scar almost impossible to heal.

DAVID COLE

Another major trail impact caused by hikers occurs when they encounter other visitors. The result: less solitude for both your group and the other party. Encountering others often detracts from the user's wilderness experience. The impact of this situation can be lessened if you follow a few simple techniques. Unless regulations prohibit it, take breaks

Whenever possible, take breaks on a durable surface away from the trail.

some distance off the trail at a durable stopping place, preferably out of view. Durable stopping places include rock outcrops, sand, other nonvegetated places, and sites with
resistant vegetation, such as dry, grassy meadows. Here you
can enjoy more natural surroundings, and other parties can
pass by without noticing you.

If you do meet other hikers on a trail, move off to one side
and stop; continuing to walk at the edge widens the trail.
When you meet a horse party, allow it plenty of room, as
horses can frighten easily. Your entire group should move off
to the same side of the trail, preferably the downhill side, and
stand quietly until the horses pass. It's easier for the wrangler
to control a spooked horse if it bolts uphill rather than downhill. Sometimes it helps if one of your party talks in a low
voice to the first rider to give the horses advance notice of
your presence.

WILL WATERMAN

When traveling cross-country, hike in groups of four to six people, and spread out instead of following a single path.

Traveling Cross-Country

Leaving the trail allows you to explore the 90 percent of wildlands not accessed by most backcountry visitors. Off-trail travel can be difficult, however, and is not for everyone. In particular, it is not for those who are unable to leave minimal traces of their passage—those who hike in large groups, choose routes over fragile ground, or travel with large numbers of pack stock. When you travel off-trail in remote backcountry, you must accept a special responsibility for the greater impact you have the potential to create. Off-trail areas are special because they have seldom been visited. Trampling will change their pristine qualities, so these areas require a different attitude and commitment to extra care.

When traveling cross-country, don't blaze trees, build cairns, or leave messages for members of your group in the dirt or sand. Such markers detract from other visitors' sense of discovery.

Select a route that avoids fragile areas, particularly wet areas, unstable slopes, and areas covered by dwarf shrubs or dense broad-leaved herbs and ferns. These are the most fragile types of vegetation, and a few passes by hikers will cause lasting damage. Spend as much time as possible on durable surfaces such as bare rock, sand and gravel, snow and ice, the deep duff of the dense forest floor, and other nonvegetated surfaces. Watch where you put your feet—try to step on as few plants as possible. Travel in small groups of no more than four to six people, and when not on a hardened surface, spread out rather than follow the same route and create a path. Where places are so fragile that even the passage of one person leaves a trail, it is better to walk single file so that only one lane is created. Although this may be the best you can do under some circumstances, challenge yourself to find routes that avoid such impact.

Why all this concern for avoiding plants and unstable soil and minimizing the trampling any one place receives? Most plants die if stepped on more than a few times, and unstable soils start eroding even with light trampling. Once these processes begin, the impact accelerates quickly. An obvious path soon attracts others; footsteps on top of yours kill more plants and displace more soil. Trails develop where they are not wanted. Without the careful route selection and maintenance of constructed trails, informal trails erode into permanent trenches that continue to deteriorate even without use. When these trails finally become too difficult to use, cross-country hikers move away, initiating trails elsewhere.

Studies show that for many types of vegetation, just twenty-five people per year walking along the same route leave a discernible path. Even where effects aren't immediately obvious, trampling alters plant communities, changing them in subtle ways. Damage begins with injury to plant tissues; through loss of leaves or stems, plants lose their ability to photosynthesize food. Growth slows, and plants produce fewer flowers. Reproduction declines. Plants that are most susceptible to damage become less common, and once trampling reaches levels where all plants are affected, barren areas develop.

On steep terrain, it's generally less damaging to walk on rock or snow. In the eastern mountains, however, even walking on rock can cause problems. Many rare and endangered plants grow in the crevices of rocky ridges.

You create less damage ascending steep soil-covered slopes than you do descending. Boot heels carry extra force when moving downhill, and this increases erosion. If slopes are so steep that it's necessary to dig toes and heels deeply into the surface to get a grip, some other route should be taken, if possible. Sometimes all that is necessary is to switchback your way down the slope. Spreading out on steep slopes also reduces damage. When descending loose scree, move slowly and cautiously. Rapid descents can be fun, but they move sizable quantities of scree downhill, causing erosion that would take years to occur under natural conditions.

Many of us know of places that were once little-known destinations but today are reached by webs of informal trails—the all-too-frequent result of cross-country travelers not treating pristine areas with the care they require. These places will continue to deteriorate if they receive further concentrated use. But they still have the ability to recover if they are given a rest. Shun places where user-created trails are developing, and stay off trails that managers have closed. Either go someplace else or spread out and stick to routes that show no evidence of previous use.

Respect Wildlife

The backcountry is the home of many different animals, from soil invertebrates to frogs, birds, deer, and bears. Although the potential impact of wilderness visitors on these animals varies, the principle remains the same: Respect their needs for food, water, and a secure home, and minimize the disruption of their lives. (It may be difficult to apply this principle to mosquitoes, when more than an occasional impact may be necessary.)

For most visitors, the kind of wildlife disturbance that is the easiest to avoid is that which attracts animals, causing them to lose their wildness. When Ron Rau, an Alaska biologist, reports that wolves chase pickup trucks because oil pipeline workers toss sandwiches out of windows, it's easy to criticize such behavior. Backcountry visitors, however, are often equally at fault. When a bear ransacks a camp in the Great Smoky Mountains or Yosemite National Park because someone carelessly left food lying about, the effects of wildlife disturbance hit home.

Wolves and bears may be the most glamorous animals attracted to food, but they aren't the only problem. Careless scattering of food scraps attracts ants, which have become a nuisance at many desert campsites. Some birds—such as gray jays, which are nicknamed "camp robbers" in many wildland camps—and most rodents are also attracted by food scraps, food handouts, and even food left unprotected in packs or in tents. Camp-marauding raccoons are a problem at many campsites in the eastern states. Loss of food, damage to equipment, and animal bites are some of the undesirable consequences, but the worst effect is the change that occurs in the animals themselves. Wilderness animals that lose their wildness often wind up losing their lives as well.

Although attracting animals is an obvious problem, some of the most serious visitor impacts on wildlife are more difficult to detect. Few of us realize that camping near a water hole in the desert keeps bighorn sheep away. If the bighorns don't get enough water, or if they move to less productive habitat, they will be less healthy and less likely to reproduce. Ultimately, populations will decline. We also alter the habitat of smaller animals when we disturb vegetation, alive or dead. Many small mammals and birds live in shrubbery, standing snags, and downed wood that are disturbed when campsites are trampled or firewood gathered.

Unintentional, seemingly innocuous disturbances of animals, such as encountering them along the trail or camping close to a nest or den, can have severe effects—particularly on large mammals and birds. The animals often react with excitement, alarm, and even flight, all of which consume energy needed for growth and reproduction. Animals that are healthy, well fed, and able to escape are more capable of withstanding disturbance than those that are underfed, highly parasitized, weakened by severe weather, nesting, or giving birth.

Sometimes animals seem unconcerned even when approached closely, whereas other times they disappear in a flash when you come in sight. Animals tend to be disturbed by unexpected and unpredictable events; quick movements and loud noises are particularly stressful. Animals that are regularly disturbed by visitors are more likely to tolerate your intrusion than those that have had little previous contact with humans. In Yellowstone National Park, for example, elk that live close to the town of Mammoth Hot Springs typically do not flee until cross-country skiers get within fifty feet. In more remote parts of the park, however, elk take flight when skiers are as much as a quarter mile away. Studies elsewhere have shown that hikers who stayed on trails disturbed marmots less than those who left the trails.

Coyote

Animals are particularly vulnerable to disturbances that are reminiscent of interactions with predators or that block their escape routes. For example, a person suddenly appearing over a ridge will cause bighorn sheep to flee, yet humans approaching from below are often watched with little concern. When dogs accompany those people, however, the level of disturbance becomes severe.

To be fair, we don't always know how stressful it is to cause an animal to flee. Sometimes they simply return a little while later, none the worse for the experience. But there are numerous situations where rapid escape is clearly harmful. Flights of pregnant animals have caused miscarriage. There have even been accounts of disoriented mammals, such as deer and elk, drowning in escape attempts. Numerous studies have shown how frightened adult birds have either abandoned their nests and young permanently or left them momentarily vulnerable to predators. Gulls, for example, eat eggs left unattended by frightened seabirds—birds of many types, from eiders and loons in New England to brown pelicans in Baja California. Some predators have even learned to follow human scent trails to nests.

Subtler consequences of flight have also been documented. Frequently disturbed feeding areas are abandoned for less productive ranges. Crowding more and more animals onto the ever-smaller undisturbed parts of our wildlands causes populations to become less healthy and to dwindle in size. The upshot will be less wildlife, one of the most valuable qualities of our wildland heritage.

What can you do? First, don't come with unrealistic expectations of close encounters with wildlife. Make it your goal to observe animals in their habitat, rather than on your terms. Second, learn about the animals indigenous to the place you're visiting. Your appreciation of the area and your chance of seeing wildlife will increase, plus your knowledge will alert you to the times of year (particularly birthing seasons) and places (nest sites, watering and feeding grounds) where disturbance is most critical. Armed with this knowledge, you can make informed decisions about where to travel and camp. Simple means of avoiding disturbance include observing animals from behind cover and at a distance, and collecting water from a spring but camping out of sight. Don't continue to approach animals when you can tell they are aware of you. At this point, their behavior is being affected by your presence and stress is more likely. Give animals a particularly wide berth during the nesting and birthing season.

Finally, be fastidious about food storage and food scraps. Don't pollute the animals' homes or teach them bad eating habits. Store food in sealed containers whenever possible. Bearproof canisters are available for backpackers and can serve to protect all forms of wildlife from becoming habituated to human food.

Wildlife should be enjoyed, but remember that you're entering the animals' home. With knowledge, respect, and a lot of care, you can avoid adversely affecting them. As always, the need for care increases as you explore increasingly remote off-trail areas. These areas are the last bastions for truly wild species. You have the luxury of choosing to visit these places; wild animals have no place else to go.

Be Considerate of Other Visitors

Most backcountry visitors prefer not to encounter other people. In a study of visitors to two western wilderness areas, Forest Service researcher George Stankey found that people were most satisfied when they had minimal contact with others. In addition, he found that the type of visitor encountered was more important than the number of encounters. Most visitors are particularly annoyed when they run into unusually large parties or people on horseback.

There are a few simple ways to minimize contact with other parties. Again, plan ahead and prepare. Whenever possible, visit the backcountry during seasons or days of the week when use is low.

Travel in small groups whenever possible. Although large parties usually represent only a small percentage of total use, they can have a disproportionate impact on the experience of the people they encounter when traveling the backcountry. In Stankey's study, most users, given the choice, preferred meeting ten groups of two to one group of twenty.

What is the optimal group size? From the standpoint of safety, a group consisting of four to six individuals is minimal, especially when traveling off-trail. In case of sickness or injury, one or two people can stay with the victim while the others go for help. A group of four to six people is also large enough for safe travel in grizzly country, while still being

Land managers have attempted to repair heavily damaged trails in New England and other areas.

small enough to minimize impact on
other visitors and the environment. Traveling in small groups is particularly
important when moving off-trail.

Large groups can reduce their impact
on other parties and the environment by
hiking and camping in smaller groups of
four to six. For large group activities such as
classes, choose a durable site that is well hidden from trails and campsites, but then split
up into smaller groups for cooking and
camping. To reduce encounters, pay close
attention to the planning element of the
trip—consider off-peak seasons, and avoid
camping at popular destinations. Group size
will vary whether people are hiking with
friends, family, or organized groups, such as
Boy Scouts or Girl Scouts. Each of these groups   *Brome*
seeks a sense of remoteness, so it's important to remember
that large groups should attempt to mimic the style of small
groups whenever possible in order to reduce both ecological
and social impacts.

Whatever the time of year or the size of the group,
whether on- or off-trail, always travel quietly. One exception,
however, is in grizzly habitat, where it is imperative to make
noise to avoid confrontations. But in places where you can
travel silently, you'll find that your senses are heightened in
the still, slow pace found in wildlands. Such a setting is con-
ducive to understanding more about the subtle rhythms and
balances of nature. If you travel quietly, you will be more
aware of your environment, wildlife will be less disturbed,
and other visitors will appreciate the solitude.

To minimize the likelihood that others will see you and
your camp, other than during hunting season, wear and carry
earth-colored clothes and equipment, particularly tents.
Although vivid yellows, oranges, and purples may be the
hues of an alpine hillside in summer or autumn, bright

human colors reinforce the feeling of crowdedness. Small objects, however, such as tent pegs or handkerchiefs, may not be visible and could be left behind if their color is muted.

Keep in Mind

Consider your route when selecting shoes. Always choose a hiking boot or shoe with comfortable yet safe support. Too often, inexperienced hikers pick a heavy, stiff-soled boot beyond the requirements necessary for the backcountry they plan to travel. One hiker, William Harlow, experimented with the amount of earth that was raised and exposed to erosion when a cleated hiking sole was pressed into wet soil. Harlow's experiment suggests that one hiker traveling one mile can leave 120 pounds of raised earth in his bootprints— earth that is ready to wash away with the first heavy rain. Although this is probably a worst-case example, it illustrates the potential damage of a lug-soled boot.

Shrubby Cinquefoil

When hiking gentle country, consider using a light pair of footwear. Grandma Gatewood, the sixty-seven-year-old woman who hiked all two thousand miles of the Appalachian Trail three times, wore a pair of sneakers. Although such light shoes are not appropriate if you are carrying a heavy pack or hiking over boulders and snowfields, bring a pair of light-weight, smooth-soled shoes to slip into once a campsite is selected.

Carry out all of your litter, and on the way out—when your pack is light—pick up a little extra. Some hikers even reserve an empty pack pocket and a plastic bag for trash found on the trail. Allow others a sense of discovery by leaving rocks, plants, cultural artifacts, and other objects of interest as you found them. Enjoy an occasional edible plant, if it is not prohibited by law, but don't deplete the surrounding vegetation or disturb plants that are rare or do not reproduce in abundance, such as morel mushrooms and many edible lilies. Traveling with dogs is prohibited in most national parks and increasingly discouraged in many other backcountry areas. A growing number of managers and users alike feel that a pet's place is in the home, not in our remaining wildlands. Arguments against dogs in the backcountry center on their tendency to chase wildlife, defecate in or near water sources, and harass other users when unrestrained. Where coyotes or wolves are found, another argument has recently surfaced: The tracks of a dog rob others of the certain knowledge that similar tracks may belong to resident wildlife. Yet many visitors feel that dogs have a place in the backcountry, especially if the owner accepts responsibility for minimizing the problems they may cause. One way to control a dog is to leash it or load it with a pack. When heavy enough, a pack will keep a dog close and restrains it from chasing wildlife. Dog feces can have adverse impact on the backcountry. Remove them from trails or campsites, and dispose of them as you would human waste. Like a carelessly constructed fire, dogs can have adverse effects and are certainly not necessary to the enjoyment of a backcountry experience. Still, when handled in a responsible manner, they are a comfort to many users and need not be a problem.

Finally, whether you travel by trail or cross-country, always keep in mind that someone else will be coming along after you. Strive to make the effects of your passage through the area invisible to them. This is the ultimate message of the Leave No Trace program. We aren't alone in our wildlands, and even though our impact may seem small, the overall effect of our presence in wilderness is cumulative.

SUMMARY

Plan Ahead and Prepare
- Know the regulations and special concerns for the area you visit.

- Choose a route appropriate for your goals and outdoor skill level.
- Plan your trip for the off-season or a weekday to avoid peak user times.
- Select the proper equipment, footwear, and clothing to allow you to travel safely and with minimal impact.

Travel and Camp on Durable Surfaces

- Follow established trails. Walk single file and stay on the path to avoid creating a wider tread or new track.
- Travel in small groups.
- Spread out when traveling off-trail.
- Take rest breaks off the trail and out of view on durable surfaces such as rock or sand, or places with resistant vegetation, such as dry, grassy meadows.
- Select off-trail routes that avoid fragile areas, particularly wetlands, unstable slopes, and places covered by shrubs or dense-leaved herbs and ferns.
- Stay off developing user-created trails to allow the area time to recover.

Respect Wildlife

- Avoid wildlife during sensitive times: mating, nesting, raising young, and winter.
- Be fastidious about animalproof food storage, and clean up leftover scraps.
- Never feed wildlife; feeding damages their health, alters natural behaviors, and exposes them to predators and other dangers.
- Observe wildlife from a distance; do not follow or approach them.
- Control pets at all times, or leave them at home.

Leave What You Find

- Allow others a sense of discovery by leaving rocks, plants, cultural artifacts, and other objects of interest as you found them.

Be Considerate of Other Visitors

- Be courteous; yield to other users on the trail.
- Step to the downhill side of the trail when encountering pack stock.
- Let nature's sounds prevail. Avoid loud voices and noises.

3

Selecting and Using a Campsite

An experienced leader in the backcountry often shows puzzling behavior as the day draws to a close. Campsite after campsite, all of which are acceptable to other members of the group, may be passed up. Perhaps this tenting area may not be the flattest, the tired and disgruntled say, but rearrangement of a few boulders will make it comfortable. Or if the nearest spring lies just beyond a muddy trail through a wet meadow, they offer to make a new path. What kind of perfect campsite is this leader looking for, anyway?

"Perfect" may not be the proper term, since seldom is a site ideal from everyone's perspective. Yet certain characteristics are generally agreed upon: level spots for tents, ample room for camp chores, water nearby for washing and cooking, deadwood for fires, protection from weather, a beautiful view, and last but not least, seclusion from campers outside your group. How do you arrange each camp to provide all these qualities? You don't. As author John Hart says, "The perfect camp is found, not made."

The more you travel in the backcountry, the more you are on the lookout for naturally comfortable, isolated campsites—those that require few alterations to be suitable. If it is true that your campsites are what you remember most about a wildland journey, then a night spent sliding down a steep slope, worrying about a leaning tree above your tent, or listening to a noisy group nearby is not soon forgotten. As your experience grows, you begin to watch for good campsites throughout your traveling day, even stopping early if you come across one that has exceptional attributes.

But simply finding an isolated and comfortable campsite is not enough these days. The site must be durable as well—durable in both an environmental and a social sense. Your campsite must not be damaged by your stay, nor should it harm the wilderness experience of others.

When Campsites Suffer

Your impact on other people can be particularly pronounced at campsites. Several studies have found that wilderness visitors are much more sensitive to meeting other groups in camp than to meeting them on the trail. Most people feel that camping near one other group diminishes their sense of solitude as much as meeting three groups on the trail.

In a 1980 survey of wilderness managers, researchers Randy Washburne and David Cole found that more than 70 percent of those surveyed listed vegetation loss and soil compaction at campsites as frequent problems. Such problems are, if anything, more severe today. Research indicates that the number of impacted wilderness campsites has increased greatly in the last few decades. For example, around ten lakes in the Lee Metcalf Wilderness, Montana, the number of impacted campsites increased from fifty in 1972 to ninety-two in 1988. Moreover, the number of highly impacted sites increased from twelve in 1972 to twenty-eight in 1988.

The initial effects of camping on an undisturbed site seem insignificant. Most visitors hardly notice them—some minor trampling of vegetation, blackening of a few rocks used to build a fire ring, or a little less firewood close to camp. With more use, however, the impacts become harder to miss. Vegetation disappears from large portions of the campsite, and the plants that survive are different from those growing just beyond the camp's perimeter. Under increased trampling stress, the organic layers of soil—surface litter, such as leaves, twigs, and needles; and subsurface duff, or decomposing litter—disintegrate and erode away, exposing bare mineral soil. This soil becomes increasingly compacted as trampling intensifies, restricting the movement of air and water to plant roots. As less water percolates into the soil, surface runoff increases. That runoff, in turn, increases erosion. Once soil erodes away, the prospects for the site's recovery are grim.

Impact can reach alarming levels. In the Eagle Cap Wilderness in Oregon, David Cole found that more than 90 percent of the ground vegetation in campsites had been destroyed by trampling. In addition, 95 percent of the trees were damaged by people collecting firewood, tethering horses, or hacking the trees with axes. What was particularly disturbing was that more than one-third of the trees had actually been cut down.

In addition to vegetation damage, soil compaction and erosion were prominent in Eagle Cap's impacted sites. Roots

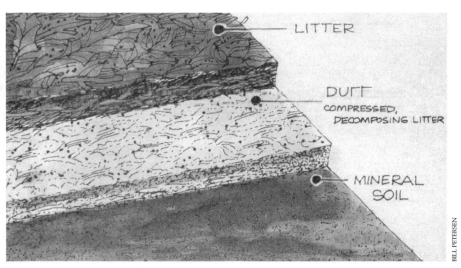

LITTER

DUFF
COMPRESSED,
DECOMPOSING LITTER

MINERAL
SOIL

BILL PETERSEN

The organic layers of soil (duff and litter) disintegrate under increased trampling, exposing bare mineral soil, which quickly erodes.

were exposed on more than one-third of the remaining trees. The campsites were large, many of them had multiple fire rings, and some sites had actually merged to form huge compacted and disturbed areas.

Such degradation happens quickly. Investigating newly opened campsites at the Delaware Water Gap—two hours outside of New York City—researcher Jeff Marion found that most damage occurred in the first year the sites were open.

Larry Merriam and his associates at the University of Minnesota found similar evidence of rapid deterioration at campsites in the Boundary Waters Canoe Area in Minnesota. Moreover, Merriam concluded that once deterioration occurred, recovery took a long time; little improvement was expected for a minimum of ten to fifteen years. Disturbed alpine areas in Colorado and elsewhere may take as long as one thousand years to recover.

Why are some campsites more seriously damaged than others? Researchers conclude that three major factors influence how much change occurs at any given campsite: the amount of use the site receives, the behavior of its users, and the site's environmental characteristics (its vegetation, soil, and topography).

Amount of Use

Common sense would dictate that of all factors, the amount of use a campsite receives is the most important—the more people using the site, the greater the impact. Actually, this is only partly true. Many frequently used sites are in much better condition than some sites used infrequently. Although almost all campsites sustain noticeable damage when camped on for more than one or two nights a year, after a certain amount of camping, careful further use doesn't have much added effect.

Studies from wildlands in such diverse locations as the Pacific Northwest, the Rocky Mountains, the Southwest deserts, the Northwoods of Minnesota, and the eastern deciduous forest all have come to similar conclusions: Additional use of sites that are already camped consistently—perhaps ten nights per year—seldom causes much further deterioration to the site itself. In the Boundary Waters Canoe Area in Minnesota, for example, campsites used fifteen nights per year lost 81 percent of their vegetation, whereas campsites used as many as seventy-five nights per year—five times as often—lost only a little more vegetation, roughly 91 percent.

These results suggest two practical choices for minimizing damage. First, in order to keep impact as small as possible, we can spread ourselves so widely that no one campsite is used more than one or two nights per year. Alternately, we can camp over and over again on the same few sites, recognizing that these places will be significantly impacted but that our impact will be confined to a very small part of the backcountry. A third option, camping on lightly to moderately impacted sites, is not a viable long-term strategy. Such sites are vulnerable to rapid deterioration with only minor increases in use—minor increases that transform lightly impacted sites into heavily impacted ones.

Sandhill Crane

An investigation at Mirror Lake in the Eagle Cap Wilderness illustrates this last point. In 1975, there were forty-two campsites around this popular subalpine lake. During the latter part of the 1970s, visitors were encouraged to avoid highly impacted campsites around the lake and find their own sites back from its shores. This attempt to disperse camping among a larger number of sites was successful, but its effects on the land were unexpected and unfortunate. The number of campsites around the lake tripled in just five years. By 1990, there were 144 campsites around Mirror Lake—sites that were as highly impacted as the original 42. If campers had stuck with the original campsites, deterioration could have been confined to those frequently used areas, leaving the surrounding land in a relatively pristine condition. In a popular place such as Mirror Lake, spreading use merely spreads impact.

Type of Use

Frequently used campsites are affected far more by what campers do when they are there than by how many times the sites are used. Campsites used by horse parties are often in worse condition than backpacker sites. In the Lee Metcalf Wilderness in Montana, for example, researcher Sidney Frissell found that horse camps were ten times larger than hiker camps, with seven times as much bare ground.

In most wilderness, the majority of groups visiting the area are small—usually between two and four people. But large groups do visit wilderness, and their potential to disturb campsites differs from that of small groups. Although the effect of party size on campsites has never been formally studied, it makes sense that a large group can cause impacts on an undisturbed site more rapidly than a small group. For example, along the New River in West Virginia, the area of vegetation loss on sites used by large commercial rafting companies was more than four times larger than the area on sites used by small groups of fishermen. At well-established campsites, however, a big group need not be a problem, as long as activities are confined within the boundaries of the existing site. The important thing is to find a site that is large enough to handle the size of your group. On pristine sites, if you are in a large group, it is a good idea to split up into camping and cooking subunits on durable surfaces to minimize impact. Activities involving all

Trumpeter Swans

members of the group can be short in duration and located on a durable site.

Campsite Location

Of the three factors that affect the severity of campsite impacts, location may be the most critical. Most people like to camp by lakes, streams, or other water sources. One study in Montana by Perry Brown and John Schomaker suggests that lakes may be the single most important factor in campsite selection. Ninety percent of all campsites had views of a lake, while only 6 percent lacked a view of any water. In the Boundary Waters Canoe Area, the most popular campsites are on islands—with water on all sides. Such findings explain why campsites in the worst condition are often found at the edge of water.

Views are also desirable at campsites. This may explain why meadows tend to be popular locations. Until a few years ago, visitors were admonished to avoid camping in meadows. Even today this is common advice. Yet recently, researchers have found that sites in dry, grassy meadows tend to be less altered by visitor impacts than those in forests. In the Bob Marshall Wilderness in Montana, David Cole learned that campsites in grasslands and open forests with a grassy understory lost less than half as much vegetation as campsites located in dense forests. In the Wind River Range in Wyoming, forested sites camped on for one night lost most of their vegetation, whereas dry, grassy meadow sites used for four nights experienced little vegetation loss. Similar findings have been reported for the White Mountains in New Hampshire, the banks of the Delaware River, and at campsites along the lakes of the Boundary Waters.

The Land Manager's Response

From this brief look at the impacts of camping and how those impacts vary with use and environmental characteristics, it should be obvious that the choice of a campsite is more complex than just finding an isolated and comfortable place to spend the night. To complicate the picture, sometimes the choice of where to camp isn't left up to the visitor at all, especially in areas that are the most crowded. For instance, land managers often prohibit camping near all wilderness water sources. In fact, many national parks and forests prohibit camping within a specified distance of all lakes and streams (usually a two-hundred-foot buffer). Many observers believe it won't be long before we see this regulation in all backcountry areas.

Other restrictions limit users to specific campsites. Thus a few areas are sacrificed so that the rest of the land remains undisturbed. Most damage occurs with dispersed use, some managers argue, and if everyone camps wherever they want, a greater proliferation of impacted camping sites will be the end result. The consequence of this way of thinking is that a quarter of our national parks allow camping only at designated sites in the backcountry. Another 30 percent of them restrict camping to designated sites in at least some parts of the backcountry.

What's the alternative if you don't wish to be told where to camp? There isn't one in those areas where numerous past visitors have acted irresponsibly and impact is severe. These places are so damaged that managers are no longer willing to risk the possibility of additional impact. They have already decided to restrict all camping—even careful camping—to certain sites. Where this decision has been made, we can only hope that it is limited to those specific places where it is necessary. For the vast majority of our backcountry lands—lands where impacts are less severe and unregulated camping still predominates—users must take responsibility before their impacts mark the land and make restrictions common fare.

Choosing a Campsite
Selecting an appropriate campsite is probably the most difficult and most critical aspect of minimum-impact backcountry

use. The choice often requires weighing conflicting variables, making trade-offs between environmental and social impacts, and using good judgment.

Your decision should be based on the intensity and type of recreational use in the area, the fragility of vegetation and soil, the likelihood of disturbance of wildlife and of other visitors, the amount of previous impact on the site and the general area, and a candid assessment of your party's potential to cause impact. All of these criteria must be evaluated if you wish to avoid causing unnecessary additional damage to a campsite. Thus, deciding where to spend the night obviously is not an easy thing to do.

Where to begin? The idea is to choose a campsite that won't be damaged by your stay. Research suggests that you'll cause the least degradation if you camp either on pristine sites that are durable and show no sign of previous use or on well-worn sites that have already been impacted to the point where further use will cause little additional deterioration. Low or moderately impacted sites (those that show obvious signs of prior use but with a substantial amount of vegetation still surviving) should be avoided. Such sites deteriorate rapidly with further use; if unused, however, they eventually recover.

When and How to Select an Established Site. Well-worn sites are the ones where most of us grew up camping—ones with prominent fire pits surrounded by compacted dirt and little vegetation. They are in prime locations—next to lakes, trail junctions, and scenic views—because they were the first sites selected when campers began using the area. Their primary drawback is that they look more like a developed campground than a pristine

Idaho Fescue

wilderness. Nevertheless, if kept clean, they make nice, impact-resistant campsites. Typically, they have lost most of their vegetation, so it is usually possible to set up several tents without having to trample any more plants or shrubs. Trails radiate to water and back to the main trail, so you can carry out camp chores without having to create new paths. Fire pits usually are in place, so you can sometimes have an evening campfire without causing further scarring.

Well-worn sites are the optimal campsite choice in areas that are popular. These places are readily accessed by trails, have many obvious campsites, and are where you expect to encounter other people. They are at the destinations mentioned in guidebooks: alpine lakes, desert oases, waterfalls, viewpoints, and trail junctions. Heavily visited wildernesses have many such places, but even remote areas may have a few.

Such popular places typically present many camping alternatives. You can select between well-worn sites, lightly impacted sites, and sites that have never been used before. Although the temptation may be strong to select a pristine or lightly impacted campsite, don't! It is always better to choose a well-worn site in popular areas than it is to risk turning a pristine or lightly impacted one into yet another hardened campsite. The proper strategy in such places is to concentrate use and impact.

When selecting a well-worn site in a popular area, look for one in a concealed, forested location with comparatively little ground vegetation, preferably in thick forest litter and duff. Try to find a flat location; not only will you be more comfortable, but you will also minimize erosion. If mineral soil exposure is kept to a minimum, soil compaction and erosion will also be reduced. If a site with thick duff isn't present, try to find one that naturally lacks vegetation and duff—one on bedrock, gravel, or sand. If possible, avoid areas with obvious soil erosion or serious root exposure. In the most popular areas, however, these may be the only sites available.

Avoid well-worn sites in meadows and on the edges of forests. Other visitors will easily see you, so social impact can be severe in these places, and they are often critical wildlife habitat as well. Camp away from water sources, trails, other campers, and scenic spots such as waterfalls and viewpoints. These places are frequented by other people, so take extra time to seek a more secluded site.

How to Use an Established Site. When setting up camp at a well-worn site, don't sprawl out. The objective is to confine impact to places that already show use and thus avoid enlarging the area of disturbance. Take care to select a site that is large enough to accommodate your group without risking damage to its edges; such damage always leads to site enlargement. Set up your tents and "kitchen" in places that

In many places, heavily impacted sites have become designated sites, such as this spot in New England.

have already lost their vegetation, where there is either barren ground or well-developed paths between tents and the cooking area. Wear soft-soled footwear when walking around camp. Step between plants rather than on them. Be particularly careful not to trample on tree seedlings. Seedlings are extremely fragile and are killed by trampling. As a result, many longtime campsites have no young trees to replace mature ones when they die.

Before leaving camp, make sure that it is clean and attractive and will appeal to the next group. Pick up litter, and clean up charcoal and other remains of fires. On many well-worn sites, it is appropriate to clean up the site and dismantle excess fire rings, as well as constructed seats and tables. Properly located facilities such as a single fire ring should be left alone, however. Dismantling them only causes additional impact, for they will most likely be rebuilt. Remember—you want to encourage others to use your site rather than to create a new one.

Camping on well-worn sites often proves frustrating if you're an experienced camper. You may feel you are just contributing to the growing problem of abuse. The truth is, there's not a lot you can do to improve a hardened site; it won't recover unless it is closed to all use for a long time. Still, there is a great deal you can do to keep the damage from spreading. Be satisfied that you're helping to decrease the total number of damaged areas by camping on just a few selected sites and by choosing ones that are the least visually obtrusive. You can encourage others to do the same by leaving the site as clean and appealing as possible. If you simply dislike well-worn campsites, plan a trip that avoids popular destinations.

When and How to Select a Pristine Site. Compared with camping on a well-worn site, use of a pristine campsite requires considerable skill and judgment. Pristine sites are those that have never been camped on before, or if they have been used, it was so long ago that any previous impact is

The best pristine campsites are located on durable surfaces, such as dry grass, snow, or rock. They show no sign of previous use and probably will not be camped on more than one or two nights a year.

impossible to detect. Pristine sites are not identifiable as campsites, and you want to keep it that way.

Pristine sites are the appropriate choice in parts of the wilderness that receive little recreational use. These are the places that are off-trail, that have few obvious campsites, and where you would be surprised to find other people. Some such areas are accessed by trails, but they are places where few people ever stop to camp. They include the bulk of wilderness lands that lie beyond the trail corridors where most people spend their time.

In the most remote places, there may be no evidence of campsite impact. Here every site is a pristine one. In other places, there may be a few places where impact is light to moderate, where people have obviously camped. Sometimes

This low- or moderate-impact campsite shows obvious signs of use, but a substantial amount of vegetation still survives. If the campfire ring is dismantled and the wood and rocks are scattered, it should eventually recover. With continued use, however, it will soon deteriorate into a high-impact site.

DAVID COLE

all that can be seen is some trampled vegetation or some scattered charcoal. Stay off these sites; let them recover.

When selecting a pristine site, make sure that it is well away from popular places and well-worn sites. Don't walk a couple hundred yards away from a lakeshore laced with impacted sites and make camp in an untouched spot. A pristine camp must be as durable as possible. Surfaces without vegetation or well-developed soils are ideal. Rock outcrops rate the best. Gravel bars, sandy beaches, snow, and ice periodically change or are removed by natural events—floods, tides, snowfall, and snowmelt—and they are also durable.

Surfaces with developed soils but no vegetation, although less desirable, are relatively durable. Your stay may cause minor soil compaction, but vegetation won't be disturbed, and recovery should be rapid. In the East, many dense forests have virtually no undergrowth, because of the lack of sunlight. Such an area is often the best choice for a pristine site. Be careful not to damage a site with sparse vegetation, however. Scattered plants uproot more easily than those found in dense mats. This is particularly true of plants growing on a forest floor. Such plants are typically tall, leafy, and spreading (characteristics that help them capture forest light) and crush easily. If you camp in a forest, choose a site with no vegetation or seek a more resistant alternative.

Dry grass is always more durable than a vegetated forest floor. Grasses (and closely related plants like sedges) often grow in mats or tufts and have tough, densely clustered leaves and stems. Grass provides a cushioning effect, and its roots keep soil particles bound together. Thus, densely matted grass meadows, if they are dry, are always better choices than forests with sparse undergrowth. Camping in such meadows may have a visual impact on other visitors, and this should be considered, but the environmental effect of a night or two of careful camping on dry grass is likely to cause less damage than a night or two in the adjacent forest.

Plant structure determines vegetation resistance. Some plants are woody; others are not. We've already discussed the relative resistance of grasslike plants to trampling. Broadleaved nonwoody plants, on the other hand, from common wildflowers to rare orchids, don't survive trampling well. Their erect, succulent stems snap off underfoot, and the broad leaves quickly shred. Woody plants seem resistant, but they, too, are often fragile. The major exceptions to this are the shrubs and trees that are large enough to avoid being trampled. Once damaged, woody plants recover slowly, and new ones usually must grow from seed. Therefore, tree seedlings and low-growing shrubs are often the most susceptible to trampling.

Studies conducted in the Cascade Mountains of Washington found that two hundred people walking through vegetation killed 90 to 100 percent of the broad-leaved nonwoody plants. The same level of trampling killed about 50 percent of the woody plants but only about 5 percent of the grasslike plants. The woody plants were more fragile than these numbers suggest, however: half of the surviving plants died within a year.

The rule of thumb for pristine sites? Always try to find a nonvegetated campsite. If you have no choice but to select a vegetated site, look first for dense patches of dry grass, and avoid vegetated forest floors or sites with low-growing shrubs.

How to Use a Pristine Site. On pristine sites, it is best to sprawl out, but carefully. The objective is to minimize the

Golden-Mantled
Ground Squirrel

number of times any part of the site is trampled. Spread out tents and cooking areas, avoid using the same routes, and move camp every night if you suspect damage to plants or soil. As you can see, these practices are exactly opposite from those used in well-worn sites. Since repeated compression of soil and vegetation is the culprit in campsite deterioration, spreading out and frequently moving should minimize impact. Wear soft-soled shoes, such as running shoes, around camp. Watch where you put your feet; take care to step between rather than on plants.

Disturbances tend to concentrate in the cooking area and in places where packs are stashed, so it is vital that these places be durable. A rocky outcrop is perfect for a kitchen or a place to prop up a pack. When you are in these activity-intensive areas or moving between them, watch where you walk to avoid crushing vegetation, and alternate your routes. It is also important to vary your path when going for water. You can reduce the number of trips you have to make to water by carrying a large, collapsible container. If paths or "social trails" start to develop, move the whole camp, the tent, or the kitchen elsewhere.

Proper use of pristine sites can be a real challenge for large groups. If not careful, such a group can create a long-lasting impact in just one night. Both dispersal of activities and short stays are particularly important for large groups in pristine areas.

When leaving a pristine site, camouflage the area by covering any scuffed-up places with duff or other native materials. If you are camping in a grassy meadow, use your fingers or a fallen branch to rake the compressed areas where tents have flattened the grass. Remember—you are trying to camouflage your campsite so that no one will be likely to choose it again. Your efforts will mitigate signs that otherwise could take days or weeks to erase.

Keep in Mind

In any kind of campsite, pristine or well worn, it almost goes without saying that you should leave the area as clean as you found it, even cleaner if possible. Never dig trenches for tents or excavate shoulder or hip depressions. Don't cut or break standing trees or branches, or pull up plants or embedded rocks to make a more pleasant camp. If you clear the sleeping area of surface rocks, twigs, or pine cones, replace these before leaving. Remember that young vegetation is easily damaged; in spring, camp on snow to avoid trampling plants early in their life cycle.

A backcountry camp always benefits from being well organized. If you have laundry to dry or equipment to air out, try to keep these items out of sight of other visitors, especially around lakeshores or open meadows. Always make sure your food is protected from animals.

Finally, stop early enough each day to choose an adequate camp. You must have sufficient time and energy to find a resistant site. Too often, tired travelers pulling in at the end of a long day on the trail shortchange themselves, the rest of us, and all our remaining wildlands by not taking the time to select a campsite that is appropriate. The approach of darkness tends to increase impact by even the most skilled and committed users. Ironically, many of these same travelers would never think of so much as dropping a piece of coconut out of their trail food.

Wolverine

Will you ever find that "perfect" campsite? Sure. They're sometimes few and far between, but they do exist. In the meantime, consider what you mean by perfect. It may mean only that you take one last look as you pack for another day of travel, knowing that whoever comes upon your campsite will never imagine anyone had camped there the night before.

SUMMARY

Campsite Impact
Three major factors influence the type and extent of campsite impact:
1. The amount of use the site receives.
2. The behavior of its users.
3. The environmental characteristics of the site (soil, vegetation, topography, and so on).

Minimizing Camping Impact
To reduce your impact, observe the following practices when camping:
- In popular areas, spreading use merely increases the area that is impacted. Camp in preexisting, well-worn sites that are large enough to accommodate your group.
- Well-worn sites can be identified by a lack of vegetation and the presence of fire rings, trails, and barren ground.
- In such areas, confine activities to the well-worn sites and avoid enlarging the area of disturbance. Leave campsites clean and attractive so that others will use them after you are gone.
- In a lightly used area, the goal is to minimize the number of times the site is trampled. Select a previously unused pristine site that is durable.
- The most durable sites are unvegetated and lack well-developed soil. Such sites include rocky outcrops, gravel bars, sandy beaches, ice, and snow.
- When it is impossible to avoid vegetation completely, consider the types of plants in the area before choosing your campsite. Grasslike plants are the most tolerant of trampling. Woody plants and broad-leaved herbs are much more vulnerable.

- On pristine sites, spread out and vary your paths around camp. Place kitchens and packs—areas that see the most concentrated use—on durable surfaces such as rock or gravel. Limit the length of your stay.
- Avoid areas where signs of impact are just beginning.

4

Fires and Stoves

Fire has long held a fascination for humans, and the realization that fire can be controllable was a first step on the long journey from our past. Rule over fire soon became important not only to survival, but also in the ability to effect change.

Even though we like to believe we are more sophisticated today, we're reluctant to lose our identity with fire. When we hike into the mountains or canoe a river, we move closer to our campfires as night falls. Campfires warm us, cook our food, and make us feel secure, stirring something deep within. They have a hold on us, refusing to burn out, even as they once held back the darkness of nights long ago.

How can anyone go camping without a fire? Ernest Thompson Seton, one of the first advocates of campcraft, insisted, "What is a camp without the evening campfire? It's nothing but a place in the woods where some people have some things." Yet today we see growing numbers of backcountry users rejecting fires in favor of lightweight stoves.

Although in some cases a lack of firewood may have forced this change, many users have made a free choice to use stoves. With the notable exception of national parks (more than 40 percent prohibit campfires), most wildernesses allow campfires. It appears that an ethic practiced by conscientious users may yet overtake a regulation before it becomes the law of the land.

If fires are so important to the camping tradition, why are people lighting up their stoves? The answer can be found from campsites on the slopes of Mount Katahdin in Maine to those on the coastal beaches of Baja: Carelessly constructed campfires leave a scar on the land. Campfire scars are perhaps the single most common and apparent impact in the backcountry. Long after grass revegetates a trampled campsite and new trees take root in an eroded switchback, the blackened smudge of a campfire tells of human use. Campfire scars continue to burn deep into wild country, lending credence to what experienced users have long advocated: Using a stove is always preferable to building a campfire.

The Dark Side of Fires
In addition to the long-term effect of blackened rocks and fire rings, campfires often cause less obvious impacts. Fires demand fuel, and when those fires are built repeatedly in one

Carelessly constructed campfires are perhaps the single most common impact in the backcountry.

area, the surrounding trees—first in the form of down and dead timber, later even living trees—show the abuse of wood gathering. In highly impacted areas, thoughtless campers often cut small trees a foot above the ground and strip larger standing trees of their twigs and lower branches. Once a tree falls, its limbs are removed, and the remainder of the trunk is axed or sawed along its length. Even soft, rotted wood is collected for the fire-building ritual, no matter how poorly it burns. Soon a campground has a "cleaned-out" look: all the wood is gone, and the repeated demand for campfires keeps it that way.

Stove users who have kicked the campfire habit not only avoid such impacts, but also profit from the freedom of a simpler life around the campsite. No time is spent gathering firewood, there is no fire ring to disguise, and finally, there is no isolation from the night world. Once the evening meal is cooked and the roar of the stove dies out, the sounds and sights of darkness return. No longer does the flickering light from a campfire divide the night into close and far, or keep a coyote or the Milky Way beyond ear or eye. Nighttime invades your campsite, your eyes gain their night vision, and you find yourself part of a larger world that would be obscured by any campfire.

Our understanding about the dark side of campfire building has increased in the past few years. A study by Dennis Fenn and associates on the effect of fires on soil found that the heat from a large campfire is capable of altering organic matter to a depth of four inches or more, with a 90 percent loss in the topmost inch of soil. The resulting sterilization of the underlying soil may at first appear unimportant, but as fire sites continue to multiply in highly impacted areas, it becomes critical. In California's Yosemite National Park, for example, more than three hundred fire rings have been reported at a single lake, many of them past scars that refuse to heal.

The use of wood to fuel campfires also can have an adverse impact on ecosystem processes such as nutrient cycling and the maintenance of site productivity. Soils are robbed of important sources of nitrogen, carbon, and organic matter, most significantly in the form of large pieces of downed wood that normally would decay slowly into the soil.

What are some of the unique roles of large downed wood? Many animals use such wood as food sources, protection, runways, and living sites. Downed logs and decaying wood serve as ideal germination sites for certain plants in what is known as the "nurse log phenomenon." They act as check dams against surface erosion, and they increase the diversity of the forest floor. But the most important functions of large downed wood lie below the ground. Decaying wood in the soil serves as a sink for energy and nutrients. It accumulates large quantities of carbon and other nutrients and releases them slowly into the soil when they are most needed. The rotting wood has a greater water-holding capacity than mineral soil and therefore can provide plants with water during drought. The wood also serves as a significant accumulation zone for soil biota, such as mycorrhizal fungi, that contribute substantially to site productivity. If fallen trees are not allowed to lie in place, decay, and become incorporated into the soil, plants, animals, and the soil will be all the poorer for it.

In the mountains, the impact of campfires increases with elevation. Studies in the Sierra Nevada have shown that forests of whitebark pine—the most common timberline forest species—appear incapable of producing enough wood to sustain high levels of firewood collection (see chapter 9).

Are Campfires Taboo?

Campfires are not taboo by a long shot in most backcountry. Although much of the preliminary evidence against fires is incriminating, many otherwise conscientious users who practice minimum-impact techniques refuse to give them up entirely. To these hikers, rafters, and canoeists, campfires are a powerful tradition and contribute much to the quality of a wildland experience. Stove converts tell redeeming tales of nighttime discoveries; campfire advocates affirm the qualities of a night held back by firelight. Listening to both sides, one concludes that no matter what further research may eventually reveal, campfires are here to stay. Many campers have a fire one night and then do without for a while. Others cook over a stove and then gather around a small fire later in the evening.

Although stoves are always preferable to campfires, there are times when fires cause little harm—if they are constructed with care. Most campfires should be considered luxuries, not necessities, especially in areas of established or growing popularity. The final rule of thumb for campfire advocates is to bring a stove and know when and where to use it.

Appropriate Campfires

Along a wild river coursing through a pristine Alaska spruce forest, at a highly impacted campground in a hardwood forest in Virginia, on a beach littered with driftwood along the Olympic Peninsula in Washington—all these locations may be suitable sites for campfires. Fires can be appropriate at both the pristine site in an area that is infrequently visited and the well-worn site in a popular area where use is concentrated. But as with camping, a fire is not appropriate at low or moderately impacted sites.

In addition to following the same criteria used in campsite selection, there are six necessary ingredients in building appropriate campfires: that they are safe, damage to the site is minimal, construction of the fire is simple, firewood is abundant, and the cleanup and camouflaging of the site are easy.

Safety. During the past two decades, research has created a dilemma for land managers, who once believed that fire was the worst fate that could befall a forest. With the growing awareness that naturally occurring fires have long been a source of rejuvenation and disease control in forest ecosystems, managers have had to amend their stand against wildfire. After scores of years and millions of dollars spent admonishing the public about the evils of wildfire, Smokey the Bear has suddenly developed a stutter. Fire can serve some good after all.

Although managers are making room in their management schemes for small, periodic, lightning-caused fires and prescribed burns, those started by human carelessness are still out of favor. The fact is that each summer, campfires escape control and burn large tracts of backcountry. Many of these tragedies could be avoided simply by using extra caution when constructing, using, and leaving campfires. Who wants to be responsible—or legally liable—for destroying an entire forest just because he or she did not take the time to use fire properly?

As a first precaution, always build campfires far from dry grass, trees, branches, and root systems, and never leave a campfire unattended. Think about what an upslope or downslope wind might do to your fire and where the sparks might fly. Avoid building fires on windy days or during periods of drought. Finally, many areas have regulations restricting the use of campfires. Be sure you know and respect those regulations. They are often issued at times when massive forest fuel buildup, coupled with unpredictable winds, gives fire the potential to cause greater-than-usual damage.

Campfire Construction in Well-Worn Sites. If you have chosen a well-worn campsite in order to limit your impact but still wish to have a campfire, you should first ask yourself whether there is enough firewood available in the immediate vicinity. If the ground has been picked clean for hundreds of feet in all directions, postpone your fire for another time and place. Otherwise you will simply enlarge the size of the area impacted by firewood collection.

If there is abundant deadwood on the ground, your next decision is where to build the fire. In popular areas where highly impacted sites are common, there is no excuse for a fire where one has never been built before; there are already more than enough fire scars in such places. Your fire should always be constructed in an existing fire ring or campfire scar. If you camp in a site that has numerous campfire scars, select the one that is the most pronounced and in the safest location.

WILL WATERMAN

In popular areas with high-impact campsites, always construct campfires in an existing fire ring or where past fires have been built.

If you are using an existing fire ring, clean out and scatter ashes in a number of widely dispersed places. Reduce the size of the fire ring until it is no more than two feet in diameter, and build the fire within this ring. If there is no ring, simply build the fire right on the ground surface already blackened by previous fires. After you're done, leave a clean and attractive site. Your goal is to encourage the next camper to use your campfire site rather than impact another site.

Campfire Construction in Pristine Sites. Choosing a location for a fire on a pristine site requires more care. Even though firewood may be abundant in the area, sloppily constructed campfires on undisturbed sites will sterilize soil and damage vegetation, especially around the fire's edges where trampling occurs. Three options to minimize the impact of fire on a pristine site, in decreasing order of preference, are to

Whenever possible, inappropriate fire rings should be dismantled and the fire scar disguised.

use a fire pan or to build a mound fire or pit fire. Fire pans, the best method, are commonly used by river runners (they are often required on rivers), but some backpackers are using them too. You can use almost any kind of metal container as a fire pan; garbage can lids and oil pans work well. Build your fire in the pan, and place it on top of rocks to help shield the ground from the heat.

Mound fires can be built almost anywhere with a few simple tools: a garden trowel, a large stuff sack, and a ground cloth or fire blanket. Building such fires is tricky and requires more time and care than building pit fires, but properly done, they cause less impact.

Mound fires are constructed on a thick pad of mineral soil laid on top of a ground cloth or fire blanket. This layer shields the underlying surface—rock, soil, or vegetation— from the heat of the fire. The first, and perhaps the trickiest, step to building the mound is finding a good source of

Motor oil drain pans make excellent fire pans and are especially popular on river trips.

DEBORAH SUSSEX

unconsolidated mineral soil. The best spots are streambeds where dry sand is exposed or in the cavity left from the roots of a fallen tree. Don't dig up mineral soil from an undisturbed place—that does more harm than good.

With the trowel, collect enough soil to build a circle several feet in diameter and at least six inches thick. Carry this back to the site in a sleeping-bag stuff sack (turned inside out to keep the inside of the bag clean). Pour the soil out onto a tarp or ground cloth. Better yet, cut an old forest fire emergency shelter or fire blanket into three-foot squares, and build the mound on top of a square. Such fire blankets provide even more insulation.

The tarp or fire blanket can be laid out on most any surface—flat rock, bare soil, or duff. It is best, however, to pick a durable site and avoid vegetation that will be flattened by the weight of the soil or trampled. The mound of soil should be circular, at least six inches thick, and have a diameter larger

Mound fires are built using mineral soil placed upon a fire cloth.

than the fire to allow for the inevitable spreading of coals. Build your fire on top of the mound. Take care to keep the fire and coals from rolling off the soil layer. When you are done with your fire and the ashes are cold, return the mineral soil to its original location.

Pit fires are built in a shallow pit. This alternative requires less construction but results in more impact and demands careful attention to location. Impact can be minimized by choosing sites that are rocky or sandy, have exposed mineral soil, or are below the high-water line along watercourses. (See chapters 7 and 8 for more details on campfire practices along rivers, lakes, and coasts.) Less desirable locations for pit fires are sites with thin duff (less than two to three inches thick) or very sparse vegetation. Never build a fire in duff more than four inches thick; the danger that the fire will spread is great in such organic soils. Avoid fires in any kind of vegetation—brush, grass, or young trees—unless it is so sparse that there is no chance you will damage plants by fire-site construction or trampling.

Decades ago, pit fires were all NOLS recommended. These fires were elaborate creations often constructed in vegetated areas. Diligent care was taken to replace the original surface vegetation exactly as it had been removed. These sites were watered in an effort to enhance their recovery. Investigation of these campfires after use, however, revealed not only damaged vegetation surrounding the site, but also sunken depressions where the pits had been. Moreover, animals often excavated these old fire pits, even though no solid food had been deposited there. Regardless of the precautions we took, pit fires continued to live up to their inglorious name.

The solution? We had the basic premise right, but the secret was to dig the pit in the correct location. Our practices soon evolved into building pit fires only in places with exposed mineral or sandy soil, avoiding vegetated areas entirely.

In gravel or mineral soil, the fire can be built directly on the soil surface. Unless the fire is very small and short-lived,

The soil is spread out over the cloth, providing enough insulation to protect the ground below.

however, a shallow pit makes it easier to camouflage the site when you leave. Where there is duff and litter, the pit serves the additional purpose of reducing fire danger. First scrape away the duff and litter from the surface down to mineral soil; then simply dig or scrape a shallow pit several inches deep. Build your fire in this shallow pit. A wide pit will minimize the chance that fire may spread. When you are done with the fire and the ashes are cold, clean out the pit, fill it in, and scatter duff on the surface as camouflage.

Finally, regardless of the construction, consider carrying a small grate if you plan to cook on a fire. Grates with metal legs prevent blackening of the rocks used for a base. They also keep pots from spilling, dousing firewood, and creating charcoal that otherwise would bum down to ash.

Firewood. Although availability of firewood is an important characteristic of an ideal campsite, there is considerable disagreement over what constitutes an adequate supply. The

BRENT HANCHETT

After the fire, the mineral soil is returned to its original location.

best firewood is small in diameter (one or two inches thick)
and found lying loose on the ground, not attached to down
timber. Never collect wood from standing trees. Small pieces
of wood are easier to burn to ash and are less critical to the
ecosystem. If wood isn't small and dry enough to break by
hand, it won't burn completely and should not be used.
(Thus, you can leave your saw or ax at home.) Avoid using
rotten wood. Although decaying wood usually makes for
undesirable firewood, too often it has been used for fuel in
highly impacted campsites. As mentioned earlier, a consen-
sus is growing among researchers that decaying, rotting
wood is critical to healthy forests. Smaller pieces of wood
contain much less of the ecosystem's nutrients and organic
matter, so burning them has less effect on site productivity.

Gather firewood away from your camp, and always leave
some wood on the ground. Regardless of size, some woody
matter is needed to maintain healthy ecosystems. The best

option is to pick up wood as you travel along the trail; usually you will find that it is more plentiful there than around established sites. You can often minimize time and effort by walking one hundred yards away from your campsite before beginning to collect wood, rather than scrounging for the few pieces others might have left closer to camp. Collect only enough wood for a small fire; don't stockpile more than you plan to use. Finally, avoid burning food scraps and plastic. A Sierra Club study headed by H. T. Harvey found that incinerating leftover food required nearly 30 percent more wood than cooking it to begin with. Burning anything other than firewood makes combustion difficult, wastes wood, transfers large quantities of heat into the soil, and makes cleanup difficult.

Cleanup. Wise site selection and good campfire construction are meaningless without a thorough cleanup, for which you must allow sufficient time. Too often, a shabby job of cleaning a campfire site is related to how late you linger in your sleeping bag. Plan ahead, and don't be in a rush to leave camp. Even better, avoid a morning fire entirely by using your stove. If your campfire burned out completely the night before, the ashes will be cold, no water will be necessary to douse the fire, and cleanup will be easier.

Whether you use a pristine site or an established fire ring, burn all wood and charcoal to ash at least thirty minutes before time to leave camp. Heap larger, partially burned pieces of wood where the heat is greatest; add small pieces to keep the fire hot until only white ash remains. Crush any leftover charcoal. If you did try to burn anything other than wood, pick out any remnants (aluminum, tin cans, food scraps) and pack them out. If necessary, cool the ash by sprinkling it with water and stirring it. When you can sift your fingers through the ash and powder, your fire is out. Scatter these remains and any unburned firewood far from the site, and distribute them over a large area so that no sign of your fire is noticeable.

If you built your campfire in an existing ring on a well-worn site, that's all the cleanup that is necessary. If multiple fire rings exist at your campsite, however, take extra time to dismantle them. Leave only a single, clean fire ring to attract the next user. (Always leave at least one fire ring in these sites; otherwise they'll most likely be built again, perhaps in a worse location.) Grind any leftover charcoal found in these fire rings to powder, and scatter it away from the site; do the same with large quantities of ash. Any blackened rocks should be returned to their original locations. If this isn't possible, scatter the rocks some distance from camp or toss them into a river or lake. The effect of your cleanup will more than compensate for the minimal effect of your fire on highly impacted sites.

If you built your fire on a pristine site, your job is more involved. You will need to scatter your fire's ash widely, taking pains to avoid discovery by others. If you constructed a mound fire, scatter the left-over ash and charcoal, then return the soil to where you originally found it; if the mound was built on a rock, rinse the rock off. When using a pit, disperse the ash, then fill in the pit with the excavated soil. Finally, disperse any excess firewood, and camouflage the site with mineral soil or litter to blend in with the surroundings.

American Avocet

SUMMARY

Fires can be appropriate when they are legal and safe, and when there is abundant firewood, construction is simple, impact is minimal, and cleanup is easy. Using a stove is always preferable to building a campfire in terms of impact on the immediate area.

Minimize Campfire Impacts
- Know the local regulations.
- Avoid fires near dry grass, trees, branches, and root systems.

- Avoid building fires on windy days.
- Never leave a fire unattended.

Collecting Wood
- Be sure there is abundant deadwood in the area.
- Never collect wood from standing trees.
- Use dead, dry wood found on the ground and no more than one or two inches thick.
- Gather wood away from your camp, leaving some so that the area does not look denuded.

Fire Construction at Well-Worn Sites
- Build fire in the most pronounced and safest preexisting fire ring at the site.
- Dismantle other fire rings in the area.
- Leave the site clean and attractive so that others will use the same ring.

Fire Construction at Pristine Sites

Fire Pans
- The best way to minimize the impact of a fire on a pristine area.
- Build the fire in a fire pan—a metal container such as a garbage can lid or an oil pan.

Mound Fires
- Appropriate only where wood is abundant and you can locate a source of mineral soil.
- Require a garden trowel, large stuff sack, and ground cloth or fire blanket.
- Fill the inside-out stuff sack with mineral soil from a streambed or the cavity left by the roots of a fallen tree. Build a circular-shaped mound of soil several feet in diameter and six to eight inches thick on a ground cloth or fire blanket that has been placed on a durable surface.

- After your fire, return the mineral soil to its original location.

Pit Fires
- Appropriate only for rocky or sandy spots with exposed mineral soil, below high-water line along watercourses, or in areas with minimal duff covering.
- To build, dig a shallow pit and construct fire in the depression.
- After your fire, fill in the pit and camouflage.

Fire Cleanup
- Burn all wood to ash.
- Let the ash cool until you can sift it through your fingers.
- Crush remaining charcoal, and scatter ash and charcoal bits widely.
- Scatter unburned firewood.
- Pick up unburned food or other remnants and pack out.

All other things being equal, choose a john with a view.

—Colin Fletcher, *The New Complete Walker*

5

Sanitation and Waste Disposal

It wasn't long ago that people discovered that uncleanliness shortened life. For millennia, humans had left their refuse wherever it fell. Not until they became creatures of villages, towns, and finally cities did people make a connection between the growing heaps of trash and human refuse and plagues of cholera, yellow fever, and typhoid. In 2500 B.C., the Mohenjo-Daro of southern Asia established the first town drainage system for human sewage. Devising means of disposal of other waste products of civilization took a little longer. The Greeks built a municipal city dump in 500 B.C., and Rome even had a collection system to clean up after the gladiator games in the Colosseum. On especially festive days, some five thousand bodies of gladiators, elephants, and tigers were carted to pits at the edge of the city and left to rot.

Today, most of us who visit the backcountry return to life in a city. We live in a society that has learned that the waste products of civilization are a source of human disease and has taken steps to remove them from our close association. Consequently, we are often uncomfortable talking about waste. As urban dwellers, we accept the modern-day mystery of waste management, complete with flush toilets, a municipal septic system euphemistically termed a "water-treatment facility," and a growling metal garbage truck that comes through the alley and ingests last night's leftovers.

But where do these leftovers go? Most of us either don't know or don't want to know. For generations now, we have given the responsibility for what has always been an unpleasant task to someone else.

The problem comes when we transfer this attitude—avoiding responsibility for our waste—to the backcountry. Until recently, most of us simply discarded our refuse—from human body waste to pop-tops—and moved on. And we were thoughtless about it. If the Forest Service provided no garbage collection at a campsite, we dug a hole and buried our cans. If we found no outhouses, we chose the closest clump of trees and left our toilet paper to blow with the wind. Once we traveled on, we didn't have to deal with the consequences of our waste.

Luckily, today, although proper disposal of waste and trash is still a problem in some backcountry areas, we're cleaning up our act. Just as important, we've begun talking about it. "Pack it in, pack it out" is a popular saying now found on signs at nearly every trailhead. As longtime researcher Bob Lucas has observed, "Trash and litter in wilderness are much less common than twenty years ago, despite increased use."

Trash and litter disposal are easy. But what about in those popular areas that are visited by lots of people, where repugnant human waste is everywhere?

Backcountry Sanitation
In their attempts to change visitor behavior, backcountry managers have successfully used maxims such as, "Take only photos, leave only footprints." But by now you know that even footprints exact a heavy price from the land when too many fall in one place. Likewise, the hope of leaving only footprints when traveling on a backcountry journey ignores the simple fact that we humans regularly consume water and food and in return produce urine and feces. Unless we are willing to pack it out, which is quite difficult on multiday adventures, we have little choice but to leave our body waste

as well. (Packing out feces is, however, a requirement on many rivers and in some popular climbing and day-use areas.)

Many visitors argue that body waste is part of a natural cycle, and if other animals disregard its deposition, so should we. In the case of urine, this is generally true; it is mostly a harmless product. Nevertheless, in tropical countries where schistosomiasis is common, urine carries the infecting parasite. Urine also attracts wildlife, and these animals may defoliate plants and dig up soil in their eagerness to ingest its salts. Urinating on rocks or in nonvegetated areas far from a water source is a simple solution to both of these problems.

Solid waste is a different matter. Undeniably, wild and domestic animals defecate almost anywhere in the outdoors, and a certain amount of "natural" fecal deposition is the result. But in the case of humans, the potential for impact is almost limitless. We simply can't ignore the fact that we have the ability and the responsibility to do a better job with our disposal of solid body waste.

The problem is that fecal waste is often the medium for disease; pathogens spread from one animal to another by means of feces. After the waste is deposited, *Kingfisher* some of the most common means of transmission are direct contact with feces, contact with a contaminated insect, or ingestion of contaminated water. With so many people heading into the backcountry these days, improper disposal of human waste can produce a significant health hazard for visitors.

Water Pollution. In many wild land areas, water is a limited resource. Yet water is in demand for a variety of competing uses; it is necessary for plants and animals, and it's a focal point of most campsite activities. Life usually suffers when the quality of water declines, but those consequences are great when humans are the users. Once pathogens in sufficient quantity find a way into water, the risk of human disease increases dramatically.

How does the quality of water measure up in backcountry areas? The data are sketchy, but preliminary evidence indicates that most backcountry waters have surprisingly low levels of bacterial contamination. In one study, researchers led by Don Erman from the University of California at Berkeley investigated the water quality of Rae Lakes, one of the most popular lake basins in the Sierra Nevada. They found that bacterial levels in the water were usually low enough for safe drinking.

But if you're starting to feel smug that the research backs up what you've always hoped was true whenever you took a sip from a mountain stream, don't. It is impossible to monitor the quality of every water source, and because animals other than humans often contribute to bacterial counts, contamination can and does occur in some areas. In Grand Canyon National Park, Arizona, coliform bacteria levels are generally low except when major tributaries are in flood. The source of contamination at these times appears to be domestic livestock or wildlife. Springs and streams in Great Smoky Mountains National Park also exceed maximum permissible levels of coliform bacteria. Again, contamination does not appear related to recreational use. Another study examined water quality in a Montana watershed that had been closed to backcountry travel. Researchers discovered that contamination actually decreased when the watershed was opened to visitors, presumably because wild animals— the principal contaminators—were scared away.

It is also important to remember that coliform bacteria is only one of many kinds of pathogens found in water. In many backcountry waters, another waterborne pathogen has reared its ugly head—a devastating intestinal protozoan called *Giardia lamblia*, which causes giardiasis. Although this disease is

Lupine

usually not fatal, some victims say that before you recover, you may wish it were. Cases of giardiasis have been increasing, but it's not clear whether contamination is spreading or whether the disease is merely being diagnosed more frequently. What is clear is that water in even the most remote backcountry can be contaminated with *Giardia*. In a study of pristine streams in the Sierra Nevada, Forest Service hydrologist Thomas Suk and his colleagues found that 35 percent of the water tested had dormant *Giardia* cysts. Exactly who the culprits are—humans, domestic cattle, or wild animals, such as beavers, ground squirrels, mice, and chipmunks—is uncertain and perhaps irrelevant as far as users are concerned. What is important is that Suk's research shows that backcountry waters are contaminated to a significant degree. Moreover, the disease caused by *Giardia* will spread with further fecal contamination by both humans and other animals.

Thus, although most backcountry waters may receive a passing grade on bacterial counts, many fail miserably because of this tiny microbe responsible for an extremely painful and debilitating form of dysentery. The warnings on backcountry and trailhead signs are true: All users who don't sterilize their water are at risk, and sanitary precautions should be taken to minimize the further spread of giardiasis through human fecal contamination of water.

The Choices. The most responsible—but not always the most practical—way to deal with human waste is to pack it out. This may be relatively easy for boaters and some pack stock parties, because they can carry portable toilets. Backpackers are understandably more reluctant to take this step.

For years, many established campsites in popular areas have been either blessed or cursed (depending on your point of view) with a traditional solution to the problem of human waste: outhouse toilets. Some users favor toilets as a necessary feature; others rebel at obtrusive structures in otherwise wild country. In Montana's Bob Marshall Wilderness, Bob Lucas found that public opinion on this subject has shifted from positive to negative in the last two decades. Visitors opposed outhouses in California's Desolation Wilderness in 1970 and they still oppose them today, despite heavy use of the area. On Wyoming's Grand Teton, which attracts some 4,000 climbers each year, the national park service recently removed a 25-year-old outhouse at 11,600 feet. It was "obnoxious, expensive, and dangerous," said park rangers, who had to precariously remove the outhouse's 50-gallon bucket from the mountain by helicopter each week during the summer climbing season. Now climbers are required to carry out their fecal waste in Mylar-coated zip-locked bags. Other popular parks are following suit: climbers in Yosemite, Mount Hood, Mount Rainier, and Mount Shasta are all required to use some sort of portable waste container system.

But what about those less heavily used backcountry areas where outhouses aren't available or users aren't yet required to carry out their waste? Proper disposal here should ultimately accomplish three objectives: minimize the chance of water pollution, minimize the chance of anything or anyone finding the waste, and maximize the rate of decomposition. Some authorities suggest the use of communal, user-created latrines; others advocate catholes—individual, shallow scrapings within a few inches of the soil surface. A more recent recommendation—appropriate only in certain uncommon situations and for particular populations—is surface disposal.

The rationale for a latrine is to concentrate waste in one, properly located place, thereby reducing the risk of water contamination and accidental direct contact. Unfortunately, however, by concentrating human waste, decomposition rates are greatly reduced. This gives animals time to find, dig up, and scatter the remains, which in turn increases the chance for human contact. Moreover, if not properly sited, latrines have a high potential for causing water pollution. Latrines also create a large area of disturbed soil, not only because of their initial excavation, but because of unavoidable trampling and compaction of nearby soil. Finally, they are frequently overfilled, making it difficult to cover them properly when they are finally closed. For all these reasons, latrines have generally fallen out of favor. They may be appropriate, however, when camping with small children or when staying in a specific area with a large group for a long time. Most managers generally recommend individual catholes instead of latrines. The common belief has been that soil microorganisms located in the organic layers close to the surface decompose feces in a short time, rendering them harmless. Researchers at Montana State University, led by Ken Temple, tested this theory by burying feces inoculated with pathogens underground for a year. Their results were disappointing. Substantial numbers of pathogens survived the entire year buried in the most organic part of the soil. Furthermore, numbers of pathogens scarcely varied with either depth of burial or the type of site. Clearly, the idea that shallow burial renders feces harmless within a short period is wishful thinking; buried feces can remain a health hazard for years.

Because decomposition of waste is so slow in both latrines and catholes, some users advocate surface disposal. Decomposition is more rapid when feces are exposed to the sun and air than when buried. Unfortunately, surface disposal increases the likelihood of contact by humans or insects and, if improperly located, of water pollution as well. It takes a high degree of skill to balance the social and ecological factors associated *Clark's Nutcracker* with surface disposal. For these reasons, surface disposal is illegal and inappropriate in many places.

The Best Choice. It seems clear that no means for the disposal of human waste in the backcountry—toilet, latrine, cathole, or surface disposal—is without problems. None can be unconditionally recommended for every situation. That is why packing it out is clearly the best solution, although it's not the most practical one in most cases. Use toilets or latrines where they have been provided. In the majority of places—those in which toilets and latrines are not provided—you must juggle the goals of minimizing water contamination and discovery by others with that of maximizing decomposition.

Where use is extremely low and soils are absent, surface disposal is a viable option (if it is not prohibited), because there is little chance that someone will contact your feces before it has decomposed. To use this method, choose a site that is not likely to be visited by others, is more than two hundred feet from water, and has a dry, open exposure. Scatter or smear the feces with a rock or stick to maximize exposure to the sun and air.

In more popular places that are regularly visited by people, surface disposal should not be considered. Here it is better to bury waste in catholes. Even though decomposition is slower than at the surface, it is more important to decrease the likelihood of contact with others. When traveling in a group, remember that the main objective is to disperse everyone's waste, not concentrate it. Choose a site that is out of the way, where other people are unlikely to walk or camp, and that is more than two hundred feet (about seventy adult steps) from water, trails, and camps. Dig a hole six to eight inches deep and four to six inches in diameter. A small garden trowel is useful for this purpose. When you are done, use a stick to stir in the soil as you cover your cathole with at least two inches of topsoil, and camouflage the surface.

Although latrines are the least desirable method of human waste disposal, they may be necessary in areas where the number of disposal sites is severely limited. They may also be appropriate for long stays by large groups in popular areas. This is especially true of inexperienced campers who may be unable to select suitable sites for catholes. Dig the latrine when you first arrive in camp, and make sure everyone knows its location. A Sierra Club study of large camping groups found that selection of a latrine site was often given low priority by experienced group leaders; consequently, less knowledgeable members frequently placed the latrine too close to campsites or water sources.

Catholes are a popular backcountry way to bury human waste, but research shows that buried waste remains a hazard when decomposition is slow.

A modification of the latrine idea is to dig a shallow trench or the equivalent of a series of catholes for a group to use during an extended stay at a single site. The advantage of this technique is that an appropriate site still can be selected by an experienced person, but with a trench the feces are not concentrated in one large hole. The disadvantage is that the technique requires extensive soil disturbance and therefore is really only appropriate in areas with exposed mineral soil or unvegetated forest litter.

If you have to dig a latrine, make it wider than it is deep, but at least six to eight inches in depth to minimize the chance that it will be excavated by animals or exposed by other people. After each use, cover the feces with soil and compress with a foot or a shovel to encourage decomposition. Once the latrine reaches within about four inches of the surface, fill it, and naturalize the site. (See "River Sanitation" in chapter 7 for a description of a portable latrine method.)

Trash and Waste Disposal
In addition to natural by-products, we humans create additional waste. In the United States alone, each person produces a daily average of five pounds of garbage; over half a million tons of garbage are deposited across the country every day. With our growing mobility, it is inevitable that some of this effluent spills into the backcountry. In 1975, for instance, more than twelve tons of trash and garbage were removed from Washington's Pasayten Wilderness using pack mules and helicopters. Undoubtedly, much more was left behind. Large quantities of litter and waste are still being removed from the backcountry today.

Besides disposable food containers such as cans, bottles, and plastic, we're littering aluminum foil, toilet paper, tampons, and leftover food, just to mention some of the more commonly found items. Although antilittering campaigns have done much to raise the level of public consciousness in recent years, even the most experienced backcountry traveler is occasionally remiss. Most visitors follow the signs: Pack

Preparing and bagging food before going into the field is an excellent way to cut down on trash.

out whatever you pack in. No matter how careful we are, however, it's difficult not to lose an item or two when taking an extended journey. So the trick in this case is to minimize the chance of loss.

To do this, be careful what you pack in. Most trash can be eliminated from the start with organized meal planning. Repackage food in plastic bags instead of cans, bottles, or aluminum foil. Calculate food rations carefully to avoid leftovers. If you end up with leftovers, package it in plastic bags and either eat it later or pack it out.

Scattering food, especially large amounts such as a burned pot of rice or noodles, is inappropriate. These scraps are aesthetically unpleasing and can attract animals. Although scattering leftovers is unlikely to cause serious problems in remote places, it's always best to pack out what you can't (or won't) eat. Burial is also ineffective, because animals smell the food and dig it up. Burning food, which is

usually moist, requires an extremely hot fire. Often your good intentions will only result in a half-charred mess that smothers the fire and leaves unburned food, charcoal, and a sloppy fire pit. Grains of rice and fuzz balls from your favorite pile jacket may not completely disrupt the local ecosystem, but litter is litter. After all, with enough time, even a Buick is biodegradable. Where do you draw the line? Challenge yourself to pack out everything possible that you take into the backcountry.

One exception to our recommendation to avoid scattering leftover solid food is fish viscera, which should be scattered widely or buried in a proper cathole, out of sight of and away from campsites, or packed out. Like moist food scraps, fish viscera will not burn adequately in a campfire unless it is exceptionally hot. At high elevations, don't throw fish remains back into lakes and streams; the cool temperatures in mountain waters act like a refrigerator, preventing rapid decomposition. Viscera slowly rotting on the bottom of crystal-clear lakes and streams provide a lasting reminder of careless humanity. (See chapter 11 for an exception to this practice in bear country.)

Today, traveling light for many visitors also means doing without that recent invention of civilization, toilet paper. Even though a growing number of users are finding leaves, grass, rocks, pine cones, or snow satisfactory, others deem this too great a sacrifice. If you spend much time in popular backcountry areas, however, you'll understand why many say toilet paper has no place in wild country. Discarded, uncovered toilet paper can linger, disgusting visitors who follow and creating possible health hazards.

If you use toilet paper, try to get by with a minimum amount, and don't use perfumed kinds which attract animals. Don't burn used tissue; it rarely combusts completely and often smolders, eventually starting a fire. The best option is to put the used paper in a plastic bag and pack it out, a practice that's not as onerous as it sounds. As a last resort—and only in moist organic soil where it will soon compost—bury your toilet paper in a cathole with your feces. Remember that in dry or cold environments buried toilet paper may last for years, and animals will likely excavate and scatter it along the surface.

Tampons require extra care. They are often difficult to burn, and campfires are seldom hot enough for complete combustion. For this reason, bag them and carry them out with your other trash. Pack them with crushed aspirin or a used tea bag to reduce odor. Under no circumstances should you leave them buried in latrines or catholes for animals to dig up. Additional precautions are necessary in bear country, where burying used tampons or sanitary napkins can be a safety hazard (see chapter 11).

WILL WATERMAN

"Natural toilet paper" is an effective solution to one of the most common causes of wilderness trash. It's more comfortable than you might imagine.

Water That Remains

Water used for cooking and dishwashing is another unavoidable waste product. For years, NOLS advocated draining excess water from cooking or washing into the corner of either a fire pit or a nearby sump hole. Upon later investigation, however, we learned that the dissolved food residue attracted animals. In addition, if the campsite was used frequently, subsequent visitors often complained of flies drawn by lingering odors. Now we recommend widely scattering such wastewater at least two hundred feet from any water source and far from any campsites that are likely to be used again soon. An exception to this practice also occurs in bear country (see chapter 11). Finally, before discarding your cooking water or dishwater, always remove food scraps that can be packed out with

When bathing, carry water at least two hundred feet from any lake or stream, lather up if you use soap, and then rinse off.

your excess trash. This is easy to do if you pack along a strainer or screen. Simply pour the water through the screen, collect the food particles, and pack them out.

Another use of water in the backcountry is for cleaning. The big question when you are washing either dishes or yourself is whether you should use soap. Many who advocate using no soap cite the benefit of having one less item to carry, as well as freedom from concern about dysentery if soap residue is left on cooking utensils. Others, stressing its importance for both personal and group hygiene, can't do without soap. A few advocate compromise—soapless dishwashing and personal bathing, but washing one's hands with soap after relieving oneself.

From strictly an impact standpoint, the best solution is not to use soap in the backcountry. Even soap that is marketed as biodegradable may alter water's delicate pH balance and seriously affect aquatic plant and animal life by introducing phosphates and other chemicals. If, however, you can't (or won't) give up soap, always use a brand that is phosphate-free, and minimize the chance of soap entering a water source by keeping it well away from streams and lakes.

The best technique for bathing is to carry water at least two hundred feet from its source before lathering up and rinsing off. (Your cooking pots or water jugs are convenient water containers.) This allows your wastewater to filter through the soil and break down before returning to any nearby body of water.

Timber Rattlesnake

If your clothes need washing, consider merely rinsing them, using no soap at all. Besides its polluting effect, soap is difficult to remove from clothing, especially without warm water, and residual soap can cause skin irritation. Choose a creek or stream with a substantial flow (not a small body of water) in which to rinse your laundry. Where water flows are more meager, rinse your clothes in water carried at least two hundred feet from the water source.

SUMMARY

Dispose of Waste Properly

In areas that are not equipped with toilet facilities, packing out feces is the most responsible way of dealing with human waste. For those who choose not to do this, either because of inconvenience or impracticality, proper disposal should accomplish four objectives:

1. Minimize the chance of water pollution.
2. Minimize the chance of anything or anyone finding the waste.
3. Maximize the rate of decomposition.

4. Eliminate contact with insects and animals that may transmit disease.

Catholes

- Catholes are the best option in areas that are regularly visited by people.
- Choose a site that is out of the way and more than two hundred feet from water, trails, and camps.
- Dig a hole six to eight inches deep and four to six inches in diameter. When you are done, stir in soil with a stick, cover with two inches of topsoil, and camouflage the surface.

Surface Disposal

- Surface disposal is only appropriate in remote, very lightly used areas with little soil.
- Make sure surface disposal is legal in the area.
- Choose a site that is remote and not likely to be visited by others. It must be more than two hundred feet from water and have a dry, open exposure.
- Scatter and smear the feces with a rock or stick to maximize exposure to sun and air.

Latrines

- Latrines are the least desirable option but may be appropriate where the number of disposal sites is severely limited, where a large group intends a long stay, or with inexperienced campers incapable of selecting proper sites for catholes.
- Dig a latrine wider than it is deep, but at least six to eight inches in depth.
- After each use, cover feces with soil and compress them with a foot or a shovel to encourage decomposition.
- Fill in the latrine once it gets within four inches of the surface, and naturalize the site.

Toilet Paper

- Rocks, sticks, snow, and vegetation make good natural toilet paper substitutes. If you must use toilet paper, don't burn it but pack it out in a plastic bag; bury it only as a last resort, and then only in moist organic soil.

Trash

- Pack it in, pack it out.
- Repackage food in plastic bags before your trip to minimize trash in the backcountry.
- Plan food rations carefully to avoid leftovers.
- Pack out solid food scraps.

Wastewater

- Strain dishwater, and scatter liquid at least two hundred feet from any water source.
- Use soap far from streams and lakes to avoid contaminating water.

Special Environments

Someone once likened the North American mosaic of wilderness that ranges from the Arctic to the Tropics to a grand play made up of many different acts. Each act represents a special kind of environment, and the multitude of plants and animals that inhabit each is a special cast of characters.

If this analogy is accurate, then it follows that the conservation practices we've discussed so far allow us only a general view of the plot. Although our basic practices are appropriate in most cases, applying a single, universal technique to every situation doesn't always work.

Special environments imply special techniques, but often we lack knowledge of the effects of human impact on different landscapes. In the following chapters, this realization is painfully obvious. Most studies have been done in forests and mountains; few have addressed impacts along rivers and coasts, or in places covered by snow and ice. Although these landscapes may present special problems, they also suggest unique opportunities: tides and floods periodically cleanse shorelines; snow makes a durable campsite that is soon rejuvenated by either new snowfall or snowmelt; and travel on rivers enables us to carry out our waste.

There are solutions to the special problems different environments present. The important question we must always ask is this: Will we humans be viewed as a major character in these wildland environments, or will we play only a minor role? Our answer should always be the same: As visitors, we must keep the changes we impress upon the land to a bare minimum, allowing natural processes to play their own parts.

In the desert, when the sun returns after a rain, there are diamonds. They are found at the tips of the slender green needles of ponderosa and piñon pine. They sparkle in the sunlight and are everywhere. You are rich. But do not try to touch them, or they will slip from your fingers and be gone.

—John Hauf, NOLS Instructor

6

Deserts

Desolate, forbidding, worthless—this has long been human-kind's view of desert lands. Hardly more than a few generations ago, Daniel Webster asked, "To what use could we ever hope to put these great deserts and those endless mountain ranges?"

Today, thousands of desert travelers could answer Webster's question. As mountain trails become more crowded, recreationists are flocking to the desert to experience the solace of arid lands. With nearly one-seventh of our planet's land surface classified as arid, it's still possible to discover vast deserts relatively untouched by humanity. North America's deserts are relatively small, constituting only 8 percent of the world's total desert area, but they are geologically young and biologically diverse, and they abound in recreational opportunity. In the past decade, this recreational opportunity has been discovered. Backcountry use of Canyonlands National Park, in the colorful Colorado Plateau of southern Utah, has increased more than 70 percent since the early eighties. At Joshua Tree National Monument, in the Mojave Desert of California, the increase in use has been even more dramatic—1993 saw five times as many backcountry visitors as 1983.

There's no precise definition of where a desert begins and ends, and the distinction between arid and semiarid is seldom clear. The common denominator is clearly dryness, however. Early meteorologists considered any area receiving less than ten inches of precipitation per year a desert. Now we realize that other factors besides rainfall—evaporation, high radiation, fierce winds, and soaring ground temperatures—contribute to dryness. Still, we have difficulty defining the limits of desert. We know that true desert is a harsh land—a land of slickrock, sand dunes, arroyos, and canyons—that is immutable, permanent, and indelibly etched into the surface of dry, hot earth.

When we look closer at the ruggedness of arid lands, we find that although the desert appears tough, it is not hardened to any and all abuses we may throw its way. Because of the scarcity of water, vegetation, and organic soils, desert lands are particularly susceptible. In fact, with the exception of alpine and arctic tundra, the effects of heavy backcountry use are more severe, more noticeable, and longer lasting in dry country than in perhaps any other environment.

The Stark Desert Landscape
Before we can learn how best to minimize impact on this landscape of extremes, we must develop an understanding of how desert ecosystems work. In particular, we must recognize the unique nature of the desert's vegetation and soils. This is not an easy task, given the vast differences among the deserts of North America, which range from hot, dry deserts, such as the Mojave of California and southern Nevada and the Chihuahuan of southern New Mexico and Texas, to the cold, dry Great Basin desert and the more biologically diverse landscapes of the subtropical Sonoran desert in southern Arizona.

Despite their biological and geographical differences, these varied lands have similarities that visitors should consider in their efforts to minimize camping impacts. Looking out over a desert's vast expanse, most visitors are impressed with its sterile and lifeless appearance. Barren ground is often more abundant than vegetation, and rock and sand more common than soil. A closer look, however, reveals that even the most desolate of deserts are very much alive. In southern

Arizona, for example, the Sonoran desert is quite rich in life. From towering saguaro cactus to minute ephemeral wildflowers, there is a bounty in these arid lands uncommon in the more barren lands to the north and west. This richness results from comparatively reliable summer rains. The less abundant deserts bordering the Sonoran are characterized by dispersed islands of life and fertility surrounded by oceans of barren rock and mineral soil. Although the barren rock and mineral soil oceans are not particularly active biologically, the islands of vegetation within them can be as diverse and teeming with life as more moist environments.

The reason the land looks so stark is that these islands may occupy only 10 to 20 percent of the ground surface. This is an adaptation to the scarcity of water. Only a limited amount of biological activity can be supported by the water available. So in most arid lands, rather than there being impoverished growth everywhere, growth is concentrated. Intervening barren areas act as watersheds, funneling precious fluid to the islands of vegetation.

Because water severely limits productivity, plants must be particularly careful to conserve it in arid climates. During dry periods, they accomplish such conservation by reducing water loss. Their conservation strategies, such as shedding leaves or having thick coatings on leaves, have the added effect of cutting back on growth. This slow growth, coupled with intense competition for water, results in the sparse vegetation characteristic of most deserts—sparse vegetation that's often the culmination of centuries of development.

Saguaro

Looking at the barren expanses between islands of desert vegetation, one can hardly help but wonder how plants can grow there. Desert soils are typically poorly developed, and since large volumes of deep groundwater are rare in arid lands, it's the water- and air-retaining capability of soil that influences patterns of desert life.

In particular, desert soils have low levels of organic matter. This is not surprising, given the low productivity of desert vegetation. Slow-growing plants produce less plant litter, which translates into less soil organic matter. The absence of organic matter exacerbates problems with water conservation, because organic matter increases the ability of soils to hold water.

Topographic features of deserts also affect vegetation and soil patterns. In mountain and plateau country, bare rock is extensive, forming cliffs and areas of outcrops. Here, the richest soil and lushest vegetation are usually found along dry washes and arroyos. When rain falls, water sweeps down these drainages, depositing sediments along the mountain bases in V-shaped stretches called alluvial fans. When these fans coalesce, they form bajadas, long, sloping ramps. The soil of alluvial fans and bajadas is generally quite coarse. Vegetation grows well here because coarse soil has large spaces between particles to hold air and water.

Desert Horned Lizard

Finer sediments wash down through the bajadas into undrained basins, or playas. Here, water remains close to the surface—so close, in fact, that after heavy rains, playas may temporarily become lakes. Vegetation is sparse in playas because the fine-textured soils allow little air and water to seep into the ground, making it difficult for plants to survive.

Water as Life Giver

Water is the lifeblood of the desert. After a heavy rain, bare limbs sprout new leaves, and a brief but glorious bloom of wildflowers may cover normally barren soil. Where water funnels into washes and arroyos, floods rip out young plants trying to establish a foothold. Larger shrubs and trees often survive floods because their root systems are stronger and able to reach the permanent water supplies that exist unseen beneath the surface of dry washes. Occasionally, permanent water is available in the desert. It may occur at springs along a fault line or where a stream flows into the desert from higher elevations. In effect, the permanent water creates a nondesert environment superimposed on the arid landscape. Where plants have access to permanent water, they grow luxuriantly, and riparian zones teem with life. These streams and water holes provide a focal point for desert wildlife. They also attract humans, who not only need the water to drink, but also enjoy the shade and more familiar landscape that the existence of permanent water brings. Attesting to these areas' prehistoric use as habitations and campsites, archaeological resources are particularly abundant around water sources. Likewise, the campsites of today's visitors also cluster around water.

Life on the Dry Side
Human use affects several important aspects of desert life. First, many of the characteristics that allow desert plants to survive, such as thick leaves or sharp spines, make them fairly hard to damage. For this reason, we think of most desert vegetation as quite resistant—tough, durable, and capable of tolerating considerable abuse. There is a limit, however, and once these plants are damaged, they have little ability to recover. In more technical terms, the resistance of most desert plants to damage is high, but their resilience is low. This is a reflection of the low productivity of desert vegetation. Surprisingly, many of the cacti and shrubs in the desert are hundreds of years old. Once they are damaged, centuries may pass before a community of mature plants can be restored.

Riparian zones—along streams and around permanent water sources—respond in the opposite way. These rich ecosystems are more similar to humid environments far from the desert. Generally, the resistance of riparian vegetation is lower than that of desert-adapted plants, but its resilience is high. Human impact in riparian zones may be readily obvious, but damage is often short-lived, either because of vegetative regrowth or because of the rejuvenating effect of periodic floods.

Choosing a Route

As desert travelers, we must choose our paths carefully. The prevalence of durable surfaces such as slickrock and dry washes and the resistance of much of the vegetation create many opportunities for minimizing impact. But the generally slow recovery rates following damage, along with the extreme importance of water, make the costs of any impact unusually high.

Where are the places we'll have the least impact? The dispersed vegetation growth pattern found in most deserts

When choosing a route in a desert environment, look for durable surfaces that can withstand travel.

provides abundant opportunity for us to walk around vegetation and rich soil. Nevertheless, even the barren-looking soil between plants can be damaged by trampling. Consequently, it is always best, particularly in more popular desert areas, to stay on established trails as much as possible. Still, trails are scarce in remote desert areas, and cross-country travel may be unavoidable.

There are a number of durable surfaces that make good routes for off-trail travel in the desert. Circuitous, sandy washes or arroyos provide impact-resistant travel paths. In permanent stream bottom areas, where more moisture is available and regrowth is faster, vegetative damage is usually not long lasting. Areas of bedrock, such as the expanses of slickrock found on the Colorado Plateau, provide another highly durable travel surface. Walking on the exposed mineral soil of playas also causes little impact, simply because few plants exist there.

When off-trail and traveling on durable surfaces, keep your group small and walk abreast to avoid compacting a new trail in places where soil is forming. Remember that as the soil granules pack closer together, the soil has less ability to hold the water needed by existing and future vegetation.

Soil That Isn't

When choosing bare-ground areas for camping and hiking, desert users must watch for another feature: cryptobiotic (cryptogam) soil crusts. These fragile crusts are found worldwide in arid lands. In some places, they are inconspicuous and hard to see. In others, where they are well developed—as on much of the Colorado Plateau—these crusts form tiny, black, irregularly raised pedestals in the sand. At first these crusts appear to be just soft, lumpy soil. Close inspection, however, reveals a spongelike structure, which is really the home of a combination of mosses, algae, lichens, and fungi. Self-sustaining biological units requiring little nutrition from the soil, cryptobiotic crusts are pioneer species that grow on barren ground. In some deserts, these crusts represent 70

Camps and kitchen areas in deserts should be on durable surfaces as well.

percent of the living cover in the landscape. A critical part of the desert soil-building process, cryptobiotic crusts prepare the ground for future plant communities. They increase soil stability, reducing water runoff and erosion. They add organic matter to the soil and they can enhance the germination and establishment of higher plants.

A mature cryptobiotic garden may take as long as one hundred years to develop, but in the few seconds it takes to walk across it, the crusts can be pounded into dust that blows away with the next windstorm. In Grand Canyon National Park, David Cole found that as few as fifteen people walking over an area of cryptogam pulverized more than one-half of the crust. Other researchers have also found that cryptobiotic soil is extremely fragile. The crusts' physiological processes—which are important to nutrient cycling—are disrupted even more rapidly. This is the most fragile ground cover ever reported, and it's quite common in many desert lands.

Another fragile arid land feature is desert pavement. Found in the Mojave Desert of southern California and

The mosses, algae, lichens, and fungi of desert cryptogams are extremely sensitive to trampling.

Nevada, and in Arizona's Sonoran desert, desert pavement is characterized by a smooth veneer of varnished rocks embedded in the soil. This process requires hundreds, if not thousands, of years, and overturning these rocks results in a virtually permanent visible impact.

If you find yourself in an area of cryptobiotic crust or desert pavement, stick to expanses of rock or sandy washes. Stay on established trails or, if there's no way to avoid the pavement or crust, follow in each other's footsteps in order to create the least disturbance. (*Note*: This recommendation is counter to the general practice of spreading out when traveling cross-country. Spreading out is best suited for crossing less fragile terrain.)

Desert Artifacts

Modern-day backcountry travelers aren't the first people to find value in desert living. The Hohokam, the Mimbres, the Fremont, the Ute, and the more renowned Anasazi have occupied the Southwest deserts over the millennia. The

By following an established trail through cryptogam, these hikers are creating the least amount of disturbance.

Anasazi, for example, flourished on the Colorado Plateau about A.D. 1000, and then mysteriously disappeared a few centuries later. Many archaeologists consider them to have been almost as advanced as the ancient Maya in Central America. Today all that is left of these civilizations are their cliff dwellings, pictographs and petroglyphs, and scattered artifacts, such as bowls and pottery. Such artifacts add mystery and a sense of times past to the desert wilderness. They have survived the vagaries of climate and the forces of decomposition for centuries. But now, because of theft and vandalism, they are quickly disappearing.

Despite the threat of stiff fines and prosecution, land managers have been unable to stem the desecration of these ancient ruins, the defacement of rock art, and the removal of surface artifacts. By some estimates, less than 10 percent of this cultural heritage remains hidden in the mesas and canyons of the Southwest.

GLENN GOODRICH

Ancient Anasazi artifacts of the Southwest are in increasing danger from curious backcountry visitors as well as thieves and vandals.

If you come across ancient dwellings in your wanderings, whether in the desert or in other environments, treat them with respect. Many of these dwellings haven't been inventoried or researched, and your disturbance will cheat others of their heritage. It is always best to view the ruins from a distance. People may say, "There's just a few of us and it's just this one time," but thousands of people making the same rationalization can cause tremendous impact.

If you do enter a cultural site, explore it with great care. If there is an established trail, stay on it. Try to locate the midden area, or "trash pile," so that you can avoid it. Middens contain important archaeological artifacts. They are usually located in front of the ruin and are extremely fragile. Never climb on roofs or walls, and do not build fires or camp inside ruins.

Finding a panel of rock art is one of the great joys of desert travel. Rock art is great for viewing, photographing, and sketching. But resist touching it or doing a tracing. Any direct contact accelerates the process of disintegration. Also, body oils stain and damage the artwork.

Campsite Selection and Use

Little is known about campsite impact in the desert, although there's a sizable body of literature on other arid land damage, especially that caused by off-road vehicles. It seems safe to assume, however, that the conclusions we've drawn about the complex interaction of desert soil, water, and vegetation also hold true for those places where our concentrated impact is greatest.

In chapter 3 we stated that established campsites tend to be expansive. In deserts, however, they are generally much smaller, sometimes averaging only a fraction of the size of campsites in forested backcountry. Why the difference? First, the smaller size of campsites in deserts is the fortuitous result of a hostile environment offering few comfortable places to camp; the terrain is often too rough to spread out. Second, desert camping is a relatively recent phenomenon; most desert areas have little or no history of deleterious "frontier-style" camping.

A third reason for smaller campsites is the inherent resistance of desert vegetation. Although few plants survive at the core of most desert campsites, the area immediately adjacent to this barren center remains relatively undisturbed. In comparison, the disturbed area surrounding campsites in more temperate climates is often nine times the size of the campsite core. Rugged plants that have evolved in the harsh desert environment resist trampling by humans. Many annuals complete their life cycle in a time period sufficiently short to avoid most recreational disturbance. Drought-enduring perennial species have small leaves with thick cuticles and often are armed with thorns or spines that keep most users away. Finally, many aboveground arid plants are small in proportion to

Desert Tortoise

their large root systems, making contact with the plant less likely.

All this may be good news for desert campsites, but resistance of vegetation to trampling is only half the story. On campsites in moister, forested environments, there's usually a lag between the time a campsite first loses vegetation and when it finally loses its organic soil. On desert campsites with little organic soil, exposure of mineral soil occurs almost as rapidly as plant cover loss. Thus, although the area of disturbance in most desert campsites is small, the magnitude of disturbance on these small sites can be extreme.

What does all of this imply for desert backcountry users choosing campsites? In popular desert areas, or when you can't be certain that you'll leave no evidence of your stay, a well-worn campsite is the best choice. Simply confine your traffic and activities to places that have already been impacted.

In more remote, lightly used desert areas, a pristine campsite is a good choice provided it is possible to avoid camping on vegetation and the site is highly resistant. Expanses of slickrock and dry washes are ideal. Camping in dry washes should be avoided, however, if there is any risk of flooding. Finally, in some places it may be possible to camp in the open ground between shrubs if there appears to be no cryptobiotic crust. This is risky, however, because some crusts are hard to discern.

Avoid moving stones to create a flat tent site. If you must remove stones, attempt to replace them before you leave, making certain not to invert them. When camping on previously unused sites, remember to keep your group size small and your stay short, and to disperse your camp activities over a wide area. Even if your group is large, you can split up the campsites and cook areas into several small groups, spreading out on durable surfaces, and thus decreasing the impacts to the land.

Desert Fires
Because of the low productivity and scattered growth of vegetation, the impacts caused by firewood collection can be

particularly severe in the desert. What little deadwood is there is important to maintaining the productivity of soils that are already low in organic matter. In popular places, there's simply not enough wood for fuel.

With this in mind, it's easy to conclude that campfires have no place in the desert. For the most part, this is true—particularly in heavily used places. In remote areas, however, there are suitable places to collect wood. Along arroyos, periodic flash floods often deposit substantial amounts of driftwood and flood debris that can be used for a campfire. It's important not to overuse this limited fuel supply, however. Wood may seem locally abundant, but often it will not be replenished until the next flash flood, which may be years away. Riparian areas, such as cottonwood groves, also may have abundant wood supplies. As elsewhere, only dead and down wood should be used. This is particularly important in arid regions, because trees and shrubs in these regions often appear dead, when in fact they are quite alive, just dry and brittle.

Provided an adequate wood supply is present, campfires may be appropriate for yet another reason. Dry desert washes often have abundant mineral soil, making them suitable locations for campfires; no rocks are blackened, no vegetation is trampled. In the morning, cold ashes can be dispersed easily by scattering them over a large area. Just covering the remnants of your campfire with sand is not good enough. Wind will blow the sand away, and the less dense charcoal and ashes will surface. Grind up any larger pieces of charcoal before scattering. Although charcoal from natural fires is relatively common in many forested areas, such is not the case in deserts, where any leftover charcoal is almost always a sign of previous camping.

Utah Juniper

Desert Sanitation

Since there is so little organic matter to provide sustenance for the microorganisms that eventually break down fecal material, sanitation in the desert presents a problem. Body waste won't decompose very rapidly in this predominantly inorganic, often sandy soil. Because deserts are hot and direct sunlight is pervasive, some advocate surface disposal in remote and little used areas. Although fecal pathogens should be readily destroyed and insect contamination isn't the problem it is in more humid conditions, surface-deposited feces are likely to remain visible for a long time in the dry air and sparse rainfall of the desert.

The best method? Shallow catholes are usually more appropriate than surface deposition. They should be located far from water and from campsites or trails. This should keep visual contact by other visitors to a minimum. Not all burial methods work in the desert, however. Here, latrines are even less acceptable than in temperate climates, for burial deeper than a few inches eliminates the sterilizing effect of the sun's heat. The number of microorganisms is so low, and aeration is so reduced because of the compact nature of many desert soils, that deep, concentrated burial only preserves solid waste. For the same reasons, toilet paper should not be buried in a desert cat hole, unless absolutely necessary; pack it out in a plastic bag.

In recent years, some visitors in high-use desert areas have begun packing out not only used toilet paper, but their feces as well. One effective, low-cost method is to carry and use a homemade "poop tube," or to purchase a device designed specifically for transporting human waste. Your waste can later be emptied in a sanitary waste disposal station. Check with local land managers or Leave No Trace, Inc., for information about these

Desert

Bighorn Sheep

products and other appropriate disposal techniques for human waste.

Water in Arid Lands

A discussion of arid country is not complete without a few cautionary words about water. In deserts where running water isn't available, a spring, seep, or water pocket is often the only supply for miles. It's critical that visitors not pollute, overconsume, or waste this valuable water; it is a finite resource.

Camping close to water is probably more appealing in the desert than in any other environment, but unless you are along a major river or in an area where water is extremely abundant, you should avoid it. Arizona law actually states that it is illegal to camp within a quarter mile of water that isn't flowing. Camping away from water will lessen encounters with other parties that might be drawn to the source. Even more important, it will give wildlife free access to water. Herein lies a problem that most desert visitors fail to consider: a water source may be only a convenience to us, but local animals depend on it for survival. Camping near water may keep away wildlife that is wary of people. For this reason, always camp well away—at least two hundred feet—and avoid using this source after dark when most desert animals are active.

When you use desert water, conserve it. It may exist only because of a lucky combination of shade, a small drip, and an occasional flood, or because inflow and evaporation are in delicate balance. Judge your type and volume of water consumption by the replenishment rate. Use small water pockets for drinking only. Springs may have enough water for you to use for washing dishes (far from the source), and flowing streams may have adequate supplies for washing clothes and bodies. But don't bathe or swim in small pools, be they water pockets of the Colorado Plateau or tinajas of Big Bend. Use only clean cups or pots to collect water. Even clean hands transfer some salt and oil into water sources.

NOLS

Water is the key to desert life, and backcountry visitors have an obligation to protect this limited resource.

Remember that there are few mechanisms for replacement or purification of these limited water sources; hence, pollution is cumulative. Overconsumption or misuse on your part will deplete water for all forms of desert life.

SUMMARY

Travel and Camp on Durable Surfaces
- Because of competition for water, desert plants grow slowly, and regrowth after disturbance can take hundreds of years. Therefore, camp in well-worn sites and travel on existing trails whenever possible.
- In pristine areas, hike in dry washes, on barren ground, or along exposed bedrock. Riparian corridors are also good travel paths, as the vegetation along streams tends to be more resilient, and the areas are often subject to rejuvenating flash floods.
- Campsites in pristine areas should be on bare rock, barren ground, or—if there is no danger of flash floods—in dry washes. Avoid all vegetation.
- When hiking and camping, stay off cryptobiotic crusts and desert pavement. These crusts are extremely fragile, and what took hundreds of years to develop can be destroyed in seconds by a few footsteps. If you must cross cryptobiotic crusts or desert pavement, follow directly in each other's footprints to minimize disturbance.
- Camp well away from water, unless you are along a major river. Use water sparingly, and avoid visiting water holes at night when animals rely on them.

Dispose of Waste Properly
- The heat of the sun is the primary mechanism of decomposition for human waste in the desert.
- Surface deposition is appropriate only in remote areas that see few visitors. Make sure feces are deposited far

from water sources—even dry water sources—and smeared thinly with a rock.

• Shallow catholes are the best option in most areas; pack out your toilet paper.

Minimize Campfire Impacts

• Fires are appropriate only in areas with an abundance of dead and down wood.

• Site fires in dry, sandy washes.

• Scatter cool ashes over a large area, and camouflage the fire site after use.

If there is magic on this planet, it is contained in water.

—Loren Eiseley, *The Immense Journey*

7

Rivers and Lakes

Water belongs to the Earth. Or perhaps more correctly, the Earth belongs to water. Outside of the planet Earth, water is solid ice or invisible vapor; only here is it found in the liquid form available for carbon-based life reactions. If the Earth's orbit were 1 percent larger, scientists speculate, its water would have frozen more than 2 billion years ago; 5 percent smaller, and it would have boiled away. Yet water is more than just the basis of life as we know it. Water transports the molecules necessary for life through leaves of plants and bodies of animals. It also forms into raindrops and puddles, rivers and streams, finally washing to the sea. On its way, water carries life to the remotest of places.

Human travel on water to gain access to wild country is nothing new, but its current popularity is. When John Wesley Powell slid his dory into the Colorado River in 1867, he could not have imagined the recreation explosion that would bring so many others to that same muddy river. In the first eighty-three years after Powell's descent down what many call the greatest river in the world, only eighty-five people followed—an average of one person each year. But in the second half of the twentieth century, people "discovered" the Colorado. In 1972 alone, more than sixteen thousand people traveled through the Colorado's Grand Canyon, and the park service responded by limiting the number of floaters. Even with this limit, the three-hundred-mile float remains one of the most intensively utilized wilderness resources in the world. Today more than twenty-three thousand visitors float the river annually, and the demand for the experience is so great that some people wait as long as a decade for a private trip through the canyon.

Such an increase in use means that minimizing the impact of visitors along the shores of both rivers and lakes is imperative. Although rivers are different from lakes, recreational use of the two is similar in many ways. On both, we travel in craft that allow us to carry more gear than most backpackers—an ability that may be good or bad for these environments, depending on what's brought and what's left behind. In addition, the use of water craft concentrates our impact along a narrow strip of land—the river or lake shoreline. But if used properly, this narrow strip of land can often be both resistant and resilient, a rare quality in wildland environments.

Rivers

When those of us who live inland from the coast think of water, we often think of rivers. Our language reflects our culture's respect for these waterways: the "mighty Mississippi," the "wide Missouri." Yet of all the forms that water takes on the Earth—oceans, glaciers, polar icecaps, lakes, groundwater, and atmospheric moisture—none take up less volume than rivers. Only one-millionth of the Earth's total water actually flows within the banks of rivers. Still, rivers are deeply ingrained in our past. We first explored the land traveling up and down their liquid highways, defined boundaries by their watersheds, and finally farmed their rich alluvial valleys. If the sea is where we came from, as author David Quammen has said, then rivers are how we got here.

Today we use rivers for more than just commerce or transportation. Between 1960 and 1982, the number of people participating in some form of canoeing, kayaking, or river running increased 500 percent—the greatest growth rate of any outdoor recreational activity. By 1987, a hefty 15 percent of the total U.S. population—nearly 36 million Americans—participated in these recreational activities. Projections for the year 2030 place whitewater boating almost another 300 percent above present levels. But though the popularity of river running has increased dramatically, the number of rivers suitable for backcountry recreation has dwindled. Dams continue to turn rivers into reservoirs, and of the three million linear miles of rivers and streams in the United States, less than 11,000 miles are classified in the National Wild and Scenic Rivers System—a meager 0.3 percent. Perhaps of even greater concern, we are just beginning to learn how to care for our wild riverine environment.

Rivers as Water Trails. At first glance, river use appears to be the nightmare of all possible backcountry situations: a large number of visitors traveling along a single thoroughfare. Compared with travel on land, however, rivers can absorb more visitor use, yet still afford each user a high degree of solitude.

River Otters

Backcountry visitors who hike seldom start at the same place or move in the same direction. Rafters or boaters on a river, on the other hand, usually begin their trip at a single location and travel in only one direction—downstream. If a group of ten people floats ten miles each day, and there are nine other such groups, each starting at the same place a day apart, every group can have a relatively unique and private wilderness experience. How many other environments exist where a hundred people can crowd onto one trail, travel ten miles each day, and be assured of not crossing paths? This ideal scenario is not always the case, however. River runners seldom move at the same pace, and use levels are rarely low enough to assure complete solitude. Nevertheless, social impacts are not as extreme as the numbers might suggest. Even in the Grand Canyon, it is possible to travel for days without seeing anyone else.

Although the social impact of heavy use might be lower than expected on river trips, the environmental impact of this use can be significant. River users usually stick to the shoreline. They may take short hikes to attractions—to a waterfall, a prehistoric site, or a hot spring—but camp is always as close to the boats as possible. This means that even when the surrounding backcountry is expansive, camping may be highly concentrated. Often, sites are few in number because of the ruggedness of a river corridor or because camping is allowed only in designated areas. Or they may be concentrated at popular locations, such as a large, sandy beach. This concentration works where river shorelines are "cleansed" by periodic flooding, causing relatively rapid recovery of campsite impacts, but above the high-water line, repeated camping can cause severe impact. As in popular mountain or desert wildernesses, repeated camping in river corridors gives certain areas a feeling of overuse while the majority of the drainage remains scenic and even pristine.

What can you do as a river traveler to lessen camping impact? If campsites are regulated, obey the regulations. On most popular rivers, camping is restricted to the few highly impacted sites that you would normally choose anyway. This serves to minimize the extent of impact and maintain most of the river corridor in a near pristine state.

If campsite selection is not regulated, follow the decision-making process discussed in chapter 3. Base your choice on the amount of use the area receives, the size and low-impact camping skill level of your group, and the availability of resistant campsites. When in doubt, it is almost always best to camp on sites that are already well worn. This is particularly important on popular rivers, if your group size is large, and if it is not possible to camp below the high-water line.

In most cases, the most resistant sites—hence the best campsite locations—are in the floodplain of the river. River users can camp on beaches, sandbars, and other nonvegetated sites below the high-water line. When the river floods, your footprints wash away, and the site appears "new" to the

DEBORAH SUSSEX

The best river camping areas are beaches, sandbars, and nonvegetated sites somewhere below the high-water line. Here, a tarp has been placed beneath a kitchen site to help reduce trampling and to catch any spilled food.

next user. If you practice floodplain camping, your impact will always be minimal.

Ground above the floodplain is less desirable, because impacts will be longer lasting and less easy to disguise. Here vegetation cover is often greater, and soils better developed. Consequently, camping is likely to destroy plants and compact soils. For example, in recent years cottonwood regeneration has been minimal along much of the Colorado River. Boaters trampling the few seedlings that do grow along the riverbank can exacerbate this problem significantly. Moreover, many of these riparian communities contain rare plant species and are extremely important habitat for animals. Still, it's not always possible to avoid high-ground locations. Dam-controlled rivers may flood daily to their high-water line, or heavy rainstorms may threaten a rapid rise in water level, forcing you to camp above the floodplain. If you must choose a high-ground site, try to select one that is already well worn. Otherwise, look for a site that is large enough to accommodate your group, has little ground vegetation, and is in a vegetation type that is widely distributed along the river.

Mink

River Campfires. Pull into a campsite on a sandbar or beach along a popular river, and you're likely to find little firewood. Heavy use by previous campers has stripped trees of deadwood, and the floating driftwood you saw in the last upstream eddy is absent. You're glad you brought your stove.

Firewood along rivers is becoming increasingly scarce. Dead and down wood, above the high-water line, has usually been picked clean around all the regularly used campsites. Consequently, it is best—and on many rivers required—to confine your wood collection to driftwood. Yet even driftwood is becoming scarce, especially on rivers controlled by dams. Little or no flooding occurs on these rivers anymore, so wood is no longer flushed periodically down the river

Concentrate use in traditional camps along popular rivers frequently used by river runners.

corridor. Dams aren't the only reason for the scarcity of fire-wood, however. Even where rivers flow free, driftwood is disappearing. River campers are burning up this finite resource more rapidly than it's being replaced. Rafters now commonly collect driftwood as they float downstream each day, since it is a sure bet that supplies will be limited close to their campsites.

If you must have a fire, one solution to the problem of insufficient firewood is to bring your own wood or charcoal. Extra weight and space are generally not a problem in a raft or canoe, and this is a simple way to have campfires for a few nights along a popular river. Again, this is a requirement on certain rivers, particularly during the warmer months of the year.

Regardless of the wood source, you must still decide where to build the fire and what to do with the ash afterward. All boaters planning on having a campfire should carry a fire

On remote rivers where fire pans are deemed unnecessary, always build campfires just above the waterline. The sand or gravel provides a durable surface, and when the river floods, all evidence will be washed away.

pan—a portable metal container in which the campfire is built and the ash confined. Garbage can lids, oil drain pans, barbecue grills, small barrels cut in half, and steel baking pans all are good makeshift fire pans. Larger and more durable fire pans are manufactured specifically for river use. Use of fire pans has been a requirement on many rivers for almost twenty years, and conscientious users take them even if they are not required. When using a fire pan, it is best to elevate it in order to avoid heat transfer to the underlying surface. Even on a sandy beach, where the heat does not cause any ecological impact, this practice will avoid sand discoloration and burned feet when someone walks across the fire site while you're dismantling camp.

When you use a fire pan, you are still faced with leftover charcoal and ash to dispose of. In the past, these fire leftovers were simply scattered around the campsite or buried in the sand. As river use has increased, however, the shortcomings of these solutions have become all too obvious. At popular campsites, white sandy beaches have slowly turned gray and then black from all the charcoal remaining from fires. Another suggested method was throwing charcoal and ash into the river. This worked fine for the ash, and it removed floating fire remnants from the campsite, but the charcoal was simply deposited in the next eddy downstream—often at another campsite. Although scattering fire remnants or throwing them in the river may not cause significant problems in a lightly used river corridor, few such rivers will exist in the future.

The best way to deal with charcoal and ash disposal is simply to pack it out. Let the fire burn down overnight, and place the cool ashes in an airtight surplus ammo box. These remains, if placed in the next night's fire, will continue to burn down so that the box rarely fills up. If you have a morning fire, cool off the ashes with a little water before putting them into the box.

River Sanitation. Human waste disposal is another serious problem river travelers face, because both riverbanks drain directly into the river, making it difficult to avoid water contamination. Burial or surface disposal well away from water may suffice along remote rivers, but it is simply inadequate on popular float trips. Especially critical are arid regions where rivers have cut narrow canyons, organic soils are minimal, and campsites are few. In the Grand Canyon— the first place where this problem was directly confronted— popular beaches began to look like latrines and smell like urinals. In 1972, more than half of river runners sampled in a study had experienced some form of gastrointestinal illness.

The solution devised by river runners for the Grand Canyon, and other popular rivers without toilets, was to carry out all solid human waste. Until recently, all the equipment needed to do this was a waterproof surplus ammo can, several large heavy-duty plastic garbage bags, chemical quicklime or Clorox, and a toilet seat. The waste was collected during the trip and then dumped in special containers near the take-out, from which it ultimately went to landfills.

Beginning in 1993, however, a new Environmental Protection Agency regulation went into effect prohibiting the dumping of human waste in landfills. This has rendered the old method of waste disposal obsolete. Now river runners must purchase a portable toilet system that can be washed out at an RV dump station or a disposal site located at the take-out. The ready-made systems can be expensive; an alternative low-cost option is to continue to use ammo cans—without plastic garbage bags—which can be emptied and washed out at the take-out. A toilet lid may be set on the ammo can for convenience, and the can sealed after each campsite. Ask other river runners what they use, and compare methods to best suit your abilities.

Yellow Monkeyflower

With either approach, chemical additives or holding tank deodorants should be used to reduce bacterial growth and retard the production of methane gas. The amount used will depend on the type of chemical and the number of people on the trip. Toilet paper, tampons, and sanitary napkins can be deposited directly into the container.

The toilet should be the first thing set up when you arrive at camp and the last thing taken down. Since it is likely to receive considerable use, it should be located on a durable spot. For hygienic reasons, establish a hand-washing system near the toilet. One traditional method is to use a tin can with a hole in the bottom as a water dispenser, set up next to a jug of fresh water and a container of soap. This "faucet" can be hung off a branch or a rock over a bucket so that water from

PIP COE/SPARKY DONAHUE

ortable toilets used on river trips can be emptied at appropriate sites after the trip.

the can will rinse off soap into the bucket. The soapy water can then be thrown into a high-volume river or scattered on land if the river is low-volume.

Along some rivers, day-use toilets—for use when the main toilet is packed away—are also required. Whether required or not, they are a good idea on popular rivers. Feces can be deposited in paper bags and stored in something like a coffee can. The used bags are then added to the main toilet at the end of the day. On lightly used rivers, which have become quite rare in the continental United States, it's appropriate to use the cathole method described in chapter 5. Individual kayakers and canoers concerned about limited space can use the "poop tube" method described in chapter 6.

Urine is another difficult problem along rivers because of its concentration in highly impacted campsites. Where there's little rainfall to dissipate it, the offensive odor of urine tends to linger. Urinating away from a camping area usually solves this problem, but the outskirts of your camp may be the kitchen or sleeping area for the next party. Therefore, always go far away from camp, and choose a location that clearly will not be a campsite, lunch spot, or rest area for someone else.

Recently, another solution to urine disposal has become popular, particularly on large western rivers: urinating directly into the river or on the wet sand along shore. Advocates of this method suggest that the high volume of water will dilute small amounts of urine adequately. It is not clear, however, whether this is a good idea on low-volume rivers with clear flows. A possible compromise is to urinate on land when away from areas of concentrated use and to urinate in the river in more popular areas.

Trash and Wastewater. Trash shouldn't be a problem on a river trip, even though there's usually more of it than on a backpacking journey. What isn't burnable can be carried out in a garbage bag or a surplus ammo box. All extra food should be carried out, not scattered. Some river users spread a large tarp on the ground and eat their meals there in order to catch any food particles that may otherwise litter the site. This practice is especially useful when camping in a highly impacted campsite that you suspect will soon receive more visitors.

There is some controversy about the appropriate procedure for disposing of wastewater from cooking and bathing. On large, silty western rivers, small amounts of leftover cooking water shouldn't be scattered at the edge of the campsite; it should be deposited directly into the river. On low-volume, clear streams, however, it may be better to scatter water on land but away from the campsite. Regardless of where water is deposited, it should be poured through a fine mesh screen to remove food particles. Bag these particles for packing out.

When bathing with soap, follow the general practices outlined in chapter 5, making sure you are at least two

Beaver

hundred feet from the river and any side streams or creeks. If possible, choose a site with organic soil. In most rivers of heavy flow (not small streams), it is appropriate to bathe directly in the river. Wherever you bathe, the less soap you use, the better.

Lakes

Lakes differ from rivers in several important ways. The ease of traveling in many directions means that solitude is less likely. Relatively constant water volumes mean there's little opportunity to camp on a spot that will be rejuvenated by yearly floods. Finally, driftwood is less common on lakes than along rivers. For these reasons, camping practices are more similar to those described in chapters 3, 4, and 5. On the other hand, many lakes do have beaches, as rivers do. These make resistant campsites, although you will be highly visible to others camped around the lake. Again, traveling by boat allows you to carry more gear than a backpacker. Therefore, unless portages are too demanding, the caring user will bring a fire pan and will consider, on popular lakes, bringing ammo boxes for charcoal and human waste.

A Final Caveat

Simply because of increased demand and limited supply, many of our remaining wildland freshwater recreation areas are highly regulated by land management agencies. A future list of wilderness rivers and lakes won't include many new additions to what we have now. Already, managers of an increasing number of rivers require that each night's campsite be reserved months in advance. In this sense, as use continues to increase, recreational river and lake management may portend much of what we should expect in the future as our favorite forests, mountains, and deserts become ever more crowded. It's important to be meticulous in our treatment of wildland rivers and lakes if we want to maintain their ecological integrity and still ensure an enjoyable experience for the many people following us.

SUMMARY

Travel and Camp on Durable Surfaces

- On most popular rivers, camping is restricted to a few highly impacted sites. Obey regulations.
- Where camping is not regulated, the most resistant sites are in the floodplain. Camp on beaches, sandbars, and other nonvegetated sites below the high-water line.
- If you must choose a high-ground site, select one that is well worn, or follow the principles discussed in chapter 3.

Dispose of Waste Properly

- Most popular western rivers require river runners to carry along a portable toilet that can be emptied at an RV dump station or a disposal site at the take-out when the trip is over. On remote rivers, the use of catholes well away from water is appropriate.
- Where there is little rainfall to dissipate urine, an offensive odor tends to linger around popular campsites. In these areas, urinate on land well away from camp, or on large, popular, and silty western rivers, urinate directly into the river.
- Wastewater should be poured through a fine mesh screen to remove food particles and then deposited directly into large, silty rivers. On low-volume, clear streams, wastewater should be scattered onshore. Pack out food particles.

Minimize Campfire Impacts

- As extra weight and space are generally not a problem in a canoe or raft, fire pans should be used on all rivers.
- Collect driftwood during the day or bring your own wood or charcoal on the river with you. Avoid depleting campsites of wood.
- Pack out ash in a sealed ammo box.

There are three great elemental sounds in nature: the sound of wind in a primeval wood, the sound of rain, and the sound of outer ocean on a beach.

—Henry Beston, *The Outermost Hous*

8

Coasts

In response to the continual search for wildlands that are relatively pristine and uncrowded, exploration of coastlines—usually in ocean kayaks—has been increasing in popularity. And it is no wonder. The coastline of the contiguous United States is almost thirty-seven thousand miles long, and Alaska has another forty-seven thousand miles of shoreline. Altogether, nearly 66 percent the United States' coastline is publicly owned (mostly in Alaska), and much of it is quite remote. Add the coasts of Canada, Mexico, and Central America, and the opportunity for secluded backcountry recreation is considerable.

Interest in coastal exploration is growing, but the impact of this type of recreation is still poorly understood. Moreover, coastlines are too diverse to be easily characterized—the cool, wet hemlock forests of coastal Alaska, for example, are quite different from the hot, dry desert shores of Baja—and impacts and appropriate conservation techniques vary accordingly.

Where the Sea Meets the Land
The Tlingit of Alaska used to believe that tides resulted from a battle between the moon and the raven. The raven wins a narrow strip of land from the sea in order to feed his brother animals, only to lose it again as the daily battle ebbs and flows.

Although we think in other terms today, some aspects of this legend still ring true: the narrow strip where the sea meets the land is extremely fertile, highly productive, and teeming with life, and it has long been a fierce battleground.

The fertility of the intertidal zone results from the rapid cycling of nutrients in the form of large quantities of detritus (organic wastes and dead matter) produced by the constant battering of wind and waves.

Of all the recreational activities described in this book, coastal travel holds the greatest potential for minimizing impact to the land. Most of the day is spent on the water, and most coastline impact occurs along a narrow strip: the intertidal zone. As is the case along rivers, the impacted zone is regularly cleansed by flooding. On coastlines, this rejuvenation usually occurs twice a day, making most impacts highly ephemeral. In some places, however, significant tides twice a day are not as common, so storms and winds can be significant forces for cleansing beaches.

Use is rarely restricted to the intertidal zone or to those beaches that extend inland for short distances, however. When we travel or camp beyond the line reached by tides and storms, we must be aware that life in these areas is more sensitive to disturbance. Therefore, it's important to concentrate as many activities as possible below the high-tide line and to use the areas beyond with special caution. We also must be concerned with impact to animals such as sea otters, sea lions, seals, and the many other species that are particularly abundant along coastlines and not accustomed to being disturbed by recreationists.

Coastal Camping

At present, few of our remote coastlines receive enough recreational pressure for impact to be widespread. There are notable exceptions, however, particularly where terrain physically restricts campsites to a few popular locations. Given the resistance and resilience of sites along the coast, it should be easy to maintain their pristine character if we're mindful of what constitutes the most durable campsites.

The absence of vegetation and organic soil in the intertidal zone and inland beaches means that there's little disturbance caused by human trampling. Sand isn't very compactable, and neither pebbles nor gravel show much sign of a past tent site or cooking area. Therefore, where intertidal

Camping above the daily high-tide line but below the monthly high-tide line guarantees minimum impact, as does cooking in the daily intertidal zone.

beaches are abundant—even in popular areas where recreational use is quite heavy—it is appropriate to choose an intertidal campsite regardless of the amount of previous use or impact. There's also no need to worry about either concentrating or dispersing tents or traffic routes as long as activities are confined to the intertidal zone. These campsites can be used repeatedly and for long periods with little adverse trampling impact, even by large groups.

Although it isn't always convenient to confine all camp activities to the intertidal zone, it's often possible to limit most use within this zone, then choose a sleeping site above the high-tide mark. On many beaches, high tides leave a distinct line of debris twice daily, about twelve hours apart. Over a period of a month, tides will be the highest near the times of the new moon and the full moon. Sleeping above the highest daily tide but below the monthly high-tide mark guarantees that all traces of your campsite will soon be washed clean. Resistant sites may be found above monthly high-tide lines, but evidence of your stay won't be removed as rapidly.

If it's necessary to camp entirely off the beach, follow the general guidelines presented in chapter 3. Decide whether to choose a pristine or a high-impact site, select a resistant location, and behave in a manner appropriate to the site you select. Be careful to avoid camping in sand dunes that are in the early stages of formation. Here, sparse vegetation is just becoming established and is particularly vulnerable to trampling. Destruction causes accelerated wind erosion, which can alter the beach and dunes. Generally, sites in grass are more resistant than those vegetated with low-growing shrubs.

Fires on the Beach

Where driftwood is abundant, campfires built within the daily intertidal zone—on sand and gravel—should have no long-lasting impact. It is best to have fires only where such sites can be used; cook on a stove and watch the night sky when camping off the beach. In the intertidal zone, simply scoop a shallow pit in the sand or gravel and you are ready to build a fire. Little cleanup is required, because the next tide should wash away the fire's remains. Still, it is important to burn wood completely rather than leave large logs with burned ends.

Be cautious about using driftwood; replenishment is unpredictable and highly periodic along many coasts. What seem like enormous quantities of driftwood today may disappear tomorrow because of displacement by storms or use by other visitors. In some areas, local residents depend on driftwood for their daily cooking and warming needs. Remember that you are merely a recreationist visiting the area. Driftwood also provides a home for certain animals and is important to the completion of natural life cycles.

It can be appropriate to collect dead and down wood above the high-tide line—*if* it is extremely abundant. Regardless of the wood source, it is always best to keep fires small, use only the wood you need, and do without a fire in places where wood is scarce.

Some areas, such as Alaska's extensive "ghost forests," require special care in gathering firewood because of overuse. The "ghost forests" resulted from the Good Friday earthquake in 1964, when vast amounts of coastal land subsided, allowing salt water to inundate what had been healthy forests. The resulting groves of dead trees now bear stark testimony to this major force of change so active along the West Coast. In some popular camping areas, these groves show signs of excessive fire building by thoughtless campers. Carry a stove so that you won't be tempted to cause further visual damage.

Coastal Sanitation

Options for disposing of human waste along the coast are similar to those in other environments. Always choose a method that 1) diminishes human, animal, and insect contact; 2) encourages decomposition; and 3) protects water quality. If the area is frequently used, a portable latrine—either a group or individual device such as a "poop tube"—is the best choice. For more remote situations, use a cathole. Since soil microorganisms are most prevalent in environments of moderate temperature and moisture, soils above the tide-line in mild coastal climates usually provide relatively rapid decomposition. Waste breakdown will be slow, however, in arid environments such as the coast of Baja.

Perhaps the most important factor to consider in choosing a cathole is the chance of feces contaminating freshwater sources. This may be the case in areas where muskeg is prevalent, such as the Alaskan coast, or where the beach is surrounded by cliffs and steep terrain, such as parts of the California coast. Avoid placing your cathole in areas where freshwater contact is likely to occur before the feces have broken down.

Choose a site off the beach, at least 200 feet from freshwater, gullies, trails, and camps. Avoid sloped terrain and step carefully to avoid trampling fragile vegetation. In the Pacific Northwest and other coastal areas where numerous indigenous people once lived, watch for shell middens, ancient refuse sites recognizable as piles of seashells and often of archaeological value. If you uncover one of these piles while digging a cathole, look for another site.

In the past, we've recommended depositing human waste in the intertidal zone under extremely remote conditions. Bacteria that break down fecal material are usually abundant here. In one coastal study by Paul Godfrey on Cape Cod, bacteria were one thousand times more numerous within the intertidal zone than in the sand above high tide. But recent laws aimed at rigorously protecting water quality in many coastal communities worldwide don't distinguish between remote and populated areas, often making disposal of any human waste within the intertidal zone illegal. Thus, we no longer recommend this method.

Disposal of Other Wastes

With few exceptions, proper disposal of trash, garbage, and wastewater is somewhat easier along the coast. If you're traveling by kayak or canoe, you probably have extra space, and carrying out your unburnables and leftover food presents little problem. In remote areas where your trash will end up in a town or village that has no proper community landfill, carry your trash to a community with an adequate waste disposal facility.

WILL WATERMAN

Making sure there are no tidal pools, deposit wastewater from cooking and washing in the intertidal zone, where bacteria will soon render it harmless.

Pick up any litter you can. In particular, plastic litter should always be packed out. Plastic doesn't degrade rapidly and often floats, tangling and killing birds and mammals. Be especially conscious of plastic six-pack holders and monofilament fishing line; these often ensnare diving birds and can harm young birds when used as nesting material.

Avoid leftover food by carefully planning your meals. If small amounts of leftovers remain that can't be eaten or packed out, scatter them far offshore. Scavenging birds are abundant in most marine environments, and unlike in other backcountry environments, where wildlife habituation to human food can alter critical feeding habits, a small amount of leftover food deposited far from shore is little reason for concern. Fish remains can be disposed of offshore in a similar manner. Depositing these onshore is less acceptable, especially in frequently visited areas. Still, packing out is the best option.

Excess cooking and soapless bathing water rapidly break down if they're deposited where bacteria are most common: in the sandy, gravelly intertidal zone. Be aware, however, that tidal pools are particularly susceptible to water pollution; avoid depositing any kind of wastewater in these locations. If the area is free of tidal pools, scattering wastewater (after straining it of food particles) in the daily intertidal zone allows food residue from cooking to sink into wet sand, where bacteria soon render it harmless. If you deposit this leftover water directly into the sea, a thin surface film may form, unless there is enough wave action to dissipate it. In remote areas that have few visitors, bathing in the sea with a biodegradable soap is an acceptable alternative to confining all washing and rinsing to the intertidal zone. This is, however, an unacceptable practice where large groups repeatedly use the same site, where wave action is nonexistent, or in areas of rich tidal pool life. Remember that it's always best to minimize the use of soap and to avoid depositing sizable quantities in any water environment.

Wildlife Disturbance
Wildlife is more abundant along coasts than in perhaps any other environment. Coastal cliffs, waters, and tidal pools teem with marine birds, mammals, fish, invertebrates, and even reptiles. It's difficult to travel where the sea meets the land and not be tempted to explore, photograph, or even harvest some of these animals.

Island ecosystems can be more vulnerable to disturbances than mainland environments, and islands accessible to canoes and kayaks deserve special attention. Often an island's isolation has led to the evolution of unique organisms—endemic populations of rare plants and animals. Because they've evolved under conditions of infrequent disturbance, these organisms may have little inherent resistance and may be particularly susceptible to the presence of humans.

Approach large concentrations of birds and sea mammals with caution; when they're nesting or birthing, avoid them entirely. A single unwitting visitor has been known to destroy an entire bird colony's hatch by frightening adults at a critical time. Exposure of eggs to heat or cold may result in chick mortality if nests are abandoned for long. Even short-term nest abandonment can be fatal, because chicks are left unprotected from predators.

If you wish to get close to a colony of birds to obtain a photograph, minimize the potential for disturbance by choosing an isolated nest or animal at the edge of the rookery. Get in and out quickly, preferably without leaving a trail. Gulls have been known to follow humans, pouncing on eggs or young as soon as the frightened adults leave. Approaching animals by boat is generally less harmful than such shore-based activities as walking or camping close to nests. It's best to shoot your pictures with a powerful telescopic lens, thus avoiding any disturbance in the first place.

Marine mammals are another concern. The Marine Mammals Protection Act prohibits the harassment, feeding, or

Approaching coastal wildlife by boat is generally less harmful than when walking along shore, because it alerts animals early on to your presence.

touching of these animals. Seals and sea lions are particularly vulnerable when they are "hauled out" on beaches, rocks, or ledges. A major factor in infant mortality is stampeding and trampling by adults while the animals are on land—stampeding and trampling that can be triggered by human disturbance. In addition, seals nurse their pups only onshore, so repeated disturbance can be highly disruptive. "Haul-out" areas should be avoided.

It's always best to approach animals from an upwind direction and stay in view to alert them of your presence early on. At the first sign of restlessness, back off. Staying a discreet distance away allows you to observe animals in a natural setting and may avert a calamity. Sometimes animals appear inquisitive and watch or follow a kayak in the water. In these situations, it's appropriate to observe the animal from whatever distance it chooses, not the distance *you* choose.

Changes in the behavior of large marine mammals caused by human recreational activities range from playful curiosity to significant agitation. In Glacier Bay, Alaska, C. S. Baker and colleagues studied the reactions of both humpback whales and harbor seals to small-boat traffic. Both species showed deviation from normal behavior, although the significance of these behavioral changes to the health of the population was hard to assess. Certainly, disruption of these animals' feeding habits could be stressful. And where human traffic is frequent, the added stress may cause some sea mammals to go elsewhere.

The harvesting of marine organisms should be given careful thought. If fishing, catch or spear only what you can legally harvest and are able to eat. When diving, restrict your hunting to areas with abundant sport fish, and try to select a variety of species rather than just a few favorites. If you return to the area often, monitor the population. If many people fish there, it's probably a good indication that you shouldn't.

Shellfish are particularly vulnerable to overharvesting. Collect only from areas with abundant populations, and practice random harvesting instead of cleaning out one area entirely. When clamming, leave the smaller clams to grow, reproduce, and ensure future generations. Fill in any holes after digging; juvenile clams and other tidal flat organisms are sensitive to changes in the depth of their sand covering. If you harvest crabs and lobsters, select only the larger specimens, and take only the males. It has become increasingly popular to catch lobsters by hand because this gives them a sporting chance. If you choose to do this, take care not to break an antenna and then lose the lobster; such injury can result in death of the animal.

Local Cultures
Because coastal ecosystems are so bountiful, many indigenous people still live by the sea. Besides your environmental impact on the land and your social impact on other visitors, you often have a cultural impact on native people. It's common courtesy to seek permission before photographing natives or trespassing on native land. In places where artifacts are present, leave them undisturbed; if removed, they will lose their archaeological context and much of their meaning. Treat these people's history and culture as an intrinsic part of the surrounding landscape—the same landscape that belongs to a people who first discovered a world where ravens battled the moon.

SUMMARY

Travel and Camp on Durable Surfaces
- Concentrate impact within the intertidal zone, where daily flooding will cleanse the area of the signs of your passing.

Minimize Campfire Impacts
- Where driftwood is abundant, campfires built in sand or gravel within the daily intertidal zone should have no long-lasting impact.

- Take care to burn wood completely, and avoid leaving large logs with blackened ends.

Dispose of Waste Properly
- In remote areas, catholes above the beach are the best option.
- In heavily used areas, carry a portable toilet.

Food Scraps and Wash Water
- Avoid leftover food by carefully planning your meals.
- Deposit excess cooking and bathing water in the intertidal zone, where bacteria will break it down rapidly.

Respect Wildlife
- Wildlife is abundant along coasts and is vulnerable to human disturbance.
- Avoid animals and birds that are nesting or giving birth.
- Approach animals from upwind and stay in view to alert them of your presence. At the first sign of restlessness, back off.
- Take photos with a powerful telescopic lens to avoid disturbance.
- When harvesting marine organisms, know and abide by the local regulations.
- Catch, gather, or spear only what you can eat.
- Practice random harvesting instead of cleaning out one area entirely.

Leave What You Find
- Many indigenous people still live by the sea; it is common courtesy to seek permission before photographing natives or trespassing on their land.
- Leave artifacts undisturbed.

In the feeble light between the drawn-in houses of a winter village, you can hear the breathing of something with ice for a heart.

—Barry Lopez, *Arctic Dreams*

9

Alpine and Arctic Tundra

A frosted alpine meadow in Wyoming, the windswept peaks of New Hampshire, and the vast arctic tundra of Alaska—what do these environments have in common? Cold. Cold that has discouraged human use of the land, at least enough to forestall the dense settlement found in more temperate climates. Cold, and the human desire to avoid it, has given us much of what today we value as wilderness. It's the land no one wanted—until now.

Although most of us may not wish to reside permanently above timberline or to live buried in the darkness of an arctic winter, many of us are choosing these cold environments as recreational areas. As the more benign landscapes become crowded, we can find awesome beauty, open space, and fewer people in the treeless tundra. A pattern has emerged: not long ago, we ventured into high mountains; now we travel into distant northern lands of arctic tundra. Although recreational use of most of these fragile landscapes may not yet be as great as in the more popular lands below timberline, it is growing, and so is the resultant impact.

How do alpine and arctic environments compare with others? If fragility were measured simply in terms of resistance to impact, then the tundra would not be considered exceptionally fragile. Many of the plants that grow there are tough—they have to be. But fragility should also be assessed in terms of how long it takes for damaged places to recover.

Biologists call the area near the treeline the kampfzone, *or zone of struggle, in recognition of the severe conditions life faces at high altitudes and latitudes, such as in this alpine zone in New England.*

On this basis, alpine and arctic tundra may be the most fragile environments of all.

Climatic conditions above timberline are harsh—short growing seasons, extreme temperatures, and nearly constant winds. Plants have adapted to these conditions, but generally at the expense of rapid growth rates. Most plants grow slowly and close to the ground. Consequently, when damage occurs, it is often long lasting. Cart tracks left in 1819 on Melville Island in the Canadian Arctic by a British expedition are still visible today. With this in mind, our primary goal in this fragile backcountry is to recognize and use resistant areas so as to avoid disturbances that will take a long time to recover.

There are many similarities between the above-timberline tundra environments found at high altitude and those found at high latitude. In fact, most of the arctic tundra used by recreationists is also mountainous. Many of the same species of plants and animals inhabit both regions, bearing testimony to a time not long ago when much of North America was covered by vast sheets of ice. Although alpine tundra and arctic tundra are considered separately, in general our recommendations apply to both.

Alpine Lands

Alpine lands are those above the upper limits of tree growth in the mountains. European biologists call upper timberline the *kampfzone* (zone of struggle), in recognition of the severe conditions that trees face at high altitude. As a hiker moves up through this zone, erect trees become increasingly stunted and dwarflike. These twisted, diminutive trees are known as *krummholz*. Above the krummholz, trees disappear altogether, leaving only low-growing alpine vegetation. As you move higher still, up toward the mountain summits, deep snowfields and lichen-encrusted boulders are all you find. Summer barely reaches this land before winter follows once again.

The elevation at which the upper timberline occurs varies according to latitude, proximity to oceans, and local topography. Timberline is found at lower elevations in higher latitudes, in mountains that are closer to the sea, on north-facing slopes, in basins, and in smaller mountain massifs. Although many factors determine the location of timberline, most ecologists agree that one of the primary factors is inadequate warmth during the growing season. Alpine lands are simply not warm enough for long enough to support trees.

To minimize our impact on this vulnerable landscape, we must first recognize that people are an unnatural part of the alpine environment. Unlike the plants and animals in temperate lands, those in alpine areas evolved largely in the absence of people. But as the popularity of alpine recreation grows, this is no longer the case. Glacier National Park, which is well known for its high-altitude environment, is visited more than 2 million times each year; visitation at Rocky

Mountain National Park is approaching 3 million per year; and even at remote Denali National Park, annual visitation has topped the .5-million mark. Plant communities—usually the first to show signs of disturbance—may be adapted to their severe physical environment, but not to the onslaught of human visitors.

Impacts at high altitude are exacerbated further by concentrated patterns of human use. Most visitors come during a very short period of time, which coincides with the peak of the alpine growing season in July and August—a time when plants are particularly vulnerable to damage.

Alpine Traveling. As at lower elevations, most alpine visitors choose to hike on trails rather than strike off cross-country. This is generally beneficial to alpine plants and soils, because trails restrict trampling. In many areas, however, trails don't go to all the places people want to visit. Also, the lack of brush and tree cover at high elevations often makes cross-country travel easier than at low elevations. Consequently, people probably venture off trails more often in the alpine zone than elsewhere, and in their wanderings, they trample places that have never before felt boots.

Although hiking off-trail can alleviate problems with visitor crowding and loss of solitude, it often aggravates environmental problems, such as loss of vegetation, damage to soils, and disturbance of wildlife. In alpine areas where recovery is particularly slow, damage from off-trail trampling can be serious. Once informal trails develop, the likelihood is great that others will follow and make things even worse. Soon, webs of trails crisscross formerly trailless areas, pristine timberline basins become scarred with tent sites and fire rings, and wildlife moves on in search of ever-fewer undisturbed ranges.

Personal responsibility for leaving no trace in alpine areas is the same as anywhere else off-trail, but here the consequences of poor judgment are much more severe. Once vegetation is lost, erosion removes already thin topsoil, making recovery extremely slow. In New Hampshire's White

Mountains, regulations require that hikers stay on trails above treeline, primarily because of the damage done to the alpine tundra by cross-country travelers in the past. Working in Colorado's Rocky Mountain National Park, scientists Beatrice Willard and John Marr estimated that complete recovery of alpine tundra disturbed by informal trails would take from several hundred to a thousand years—even if never used again. We can employ all of our horticultural know-how—planting, mulching, and fertilizing—but we still can't make these places recover quickly.

On Washington's Mount Rainier, researcher Ola Edwards uncovered a troubling situation concerning the heather meadows, a common but fragile part of many alpine landscapes. Once an opening develops in the heather cover—something that happens after a plant is stepped on just a few times—the plants are unable to close the hole by spreading vegetatively. This minor disturbance initiates an irreversible cycle of erosion. Needle ice, which forms as a result of daily freezing and thawing, lifts up the soil, subjecting it to erosion. The shallow roots of heather

Golden Eagle

are exposed, and death soon follows. Small bare spots become ever larger, and if they are abundant, the result is destruction of meadows, some of which are estimated to be at least ten thousand years old.

This scenario may seem extreme, but it's not unusual. Meadows dominated by dwarf shrubs of the heath family are a common element of the alpine landscape, whether in the White Mountains of New Hampshire or the Sierras in southern California. Above timberline, seemingly innocuous changes—changes that would be of little consequence in more resilient environments—can have long-lasting effects, particularly if they thwart the specialized means by which plants and animals adapt to the harsh climate.

Although the consequences of poor judgment when traveling off-trail are severe, the alpine zone is a relatively easy place to travel lightly. Many places are highly resistant to impact. Where routes are on bare rock or snow, the effects of trampling are negligible. Dry meadows are also surprisingly resistant. Grasses and sedges tolerate moderate trampling because they are tough and wiry and because their dense fibrous roots hold soils in place. Even here, however, it is important not to step on any place too often. To minimize your impact, travel in a small party, spread out, and steer clear of places where it's apparent others have gone before.

The most critical places to avoid when traveling off-trail are moist ground and steep slopes covered with soil or vegetation, particularly low woody plants such as heathers, huckleberries, and dwarf willows. Take particular care when ascending or descending steep slopes or when crossing areas of water-saturated soils (such as below a melting snowbank); both are common at high elevations.

Although it is always easier to minimize damage by traveling on trails, some care is also required here. Often snowbanks and the muddy soils created by snowmelt block the path. It's better to cross snowbanks and mud holes directly than to create a new trail by skirting them. If you find this difficult, perhaps you should consider a lower-altitude trip or visit alpine areas earlier or later in the year.

It's especially important to stay on the primary trail tread when hiking through meadows. Parallel ruts—as many as eleven wide in some places—scar many alpine meadows. Even where parallel trails are not yet obvious, walking alongside the established trail causes damage. In Glacier National Park, for example, researcher Ernest Hartley detected changes in vegetation caused by trampling as far as thirty-three feet beyond the path, a direct result of hikers not staying on trails.

Alpine Campsites. Many of the reasons for being particularly cautious about traveling through alpine country also apply to camping there. On Mount Rainier, Ola Edwards found the fragility of alpine areas graphically illustrated around former campsites. In sparsely vegetated, boulder-strewn areas, campers had moved rocks to create more comfortable tent sites. Unfortunately, the plants around the rocks can survive only in the sheltered microhabitats the rocks create. Once the rocks are moved—a seemingly innocent act—the vegetation dies and a permanent scar is created.

Too many of our high valleys and lake basins are already covered with heavily impacted campsites. The sad fact is that these sites won't recover unless they remain completely unused for a long period of time. You can camp at these well-worn sites and not cause further impact.

Camping on a pristine site, in contrast, demands much more care. Choose a resistant surface with no evidence of previous use. Snow, ice, rock, and mineral soil are best. Dry grass and sedge meadows are moderately resistant, whereas communities of low shrubs or succulent, herbaceous plants are

The most resistant alpine campsites are found on either snow or rock.

quite fragile. Often it's possible to concentrate most camp activities on a hard surface, such as rock or snow, and set up your tent on a softer but more fragile place.

If your camp activities can't be confined to a hard surface, disperse your traffic widely, trying not to step on the same places. Avoid fragile plants, and don't use the area more than one night. If traveling with a group of more than a few people, separate into several groups, and don't congregate in one location, unless it's on a hard surface. No alpine vegetation can tolerate being stressed for long; everything you do on a pristine site should minimize the number of times the area is trampled.

Alpine Campfires. Campfires may be absent from the highest alpine areas, but their scars are all too common at timberline. Here, it's easy to see how past campers could have reduced their impact by cooking over stoves instead of fires. But there's another reason, besides the fire scars, that campfires are out of place at the upper limits of tree growth. Close to timberline, forests simply cannot produce enough woody litter to support both frequent campfires and healthy soil.

Avens

Scientists have learned that the amount of energy produced and stored in leaves, small twigs, and branches, all of which are annually discarded in the form of litter, decreases with increasing altitude and latitude. Forests surviving at their limits of growth—be they near the Arctic Circle or pushing up the slopes of Maine's Mount Katahdin—produce relatively little new plant material each year. Consequently, they also shed relatively little litter. In these cold climates, a visitor searching for firewood is competing directly with the soil for a critical source of nutrients, necessary for productive soils and healthy trees.

What does this mean to campfire builders at timberline? Instead of compromising the future of these landscapes, use a stove.

Alpine Sanitation. As in the desert, human waste disposal is difficult in the alpine and arctic landscape because the rate of decomposition is slow. Although the limiting factors of temperature and moisture may differ between deserts and alpine lands, the effect upon decomposers that live in the soil is similar: low productivity limits their abundance and activity. As a result, both deserts and cold environments tend to preserve buried human feces.

Because of slow decomposition, it is very important to choose a method and site that 1) diminishes human, animal, and insect contact; 2) encourages decomposition; and 3) protects water quality.

In general, the cathole is still the method of choice. Choose a site with as much organic soil as possible. Even if there is no organic soil, you can usually dig a hole in sand or cut a flap out of alpine sod, do your business, and then cover it to prevent direct contact with animals and precipitation.

If there is no sand or soil available, such as on expansive rock and boulder fields, and you can't sprint for a site with such amenities, you may need to consider surface disposal. In this case, deposit the feces on a flat area and smear it as thinly as possible with a stone. The sun and wind will help dry the feces in a matter of days and will, to some degree, decontaminate it. The risks are that other people, animals, and insects may come into contact with the feces before it dries or rain may wash the waste directly into the water supply. If you must use this method, be sure to stay well away from trails, and select a spot that is as far away from water as possible.

Latrines should be avoided in tundra, as a large pile of feces will decompose at an incredibly slow rate in cold, sterile soils. If your group is large, the area is popular, and surface position or catholes are inappropriate, choose a less popular route or use campsites that have toilets.

Arctic Tundra

Although alpine areas in the Western Hemisphere were the last to be inhabited by humans, the hemisphere's high-latitude lands were some of the first. Alaska was inhabited at least ten thousand years ago, yet it contains more wild country than anywhere else in the United States, with nearly 70 percent of all national parks and about 60 percent of all designated wilderness located there. Include Canada, and it becomes clear that a substantial part of North America is still largely wild. A study by Michael McCloskey and Heather Spalding concluded that more than 40 percent of the remaining wilderness in the world consists of tundra communities. As more visitors discover these lands, we have a unique opportunity to avoid some of the disturbances so commonly found in milder backcountry areas.

The climate of the arctic tundra is quite different from that of the alpine tundra. Although both are cold most of the year, arctic tundra generally has lower maximum summer temperature, more extreme variations in day length, and less-intense solar radiation. The most important distinction, however, lies in the soil: much of the arctic ground is perennially frozen.

Here, a mixture of underground ice and soil—permafrost—lies just below a thin "active layer" of soil, which thaws with the approach of summer. As snow and ice near the surface melt, water moves down through the previously frozen soil until it meets underground ice. In most areas of the world, this water would then pass into gravel and porous rock to be stored underground, but in the Arctic, water remains pooled above the permafrost barrier. Here it has nowhere else to go, so it saturates the thin layer of thawed soil. These water-saturated landscapes are extremely fragile, adding an even greater need for caution.

Traveling in the Arctic. In summer, it is difficult to walk on arctic tundra without getting your feet wet. Few trails exist in this part of the world, and cross-country hiking is often the only method of travel. Nonetheless, visitors prefer

Permafrost is permanently frozen soil found below a thin layer of surface soil, which thaws as summer approaches.

to travel on dry surfaces where they find them. Since dry, raised ground is so uncommon, and spreading out is difficult because of low but thick vegetation, cross-country hiking tends to be concentrated on a relatively few routes, along which informal trails quickly develop.

Trampling damage to the fragile lichen-rich communities that are common at high latitudes is often serious. Lichen colonies are old—some may be many hundreds of years old—and they occupy drier ground that is less subject to permafrost. Because they grow in mats and are not rooted to the ground, they're easily displaced. The actual "leaves" of lichens are brittle when dry, and they break rapidly. Their low productivity makes recovery extremely slow; scientists estimate that it takes anywhere from thirty-five to seventy-five years for lichens to recuperate from caribou grazing.

The fragility of the arctic tundra is determined not so much by what happens aboveground as by what happens to the underlying soil after plants have been trampled. When trampling damages vegetation and exposes the underlying soil, a unique phenomenon, known as *thermokarsting*, occurs. Sun warms the exposed soil more rapidly than it does soil that is insulated by a covering of plants; consequently, more permafrost melts. Because ice crystals have a larger volume than water, the volume of the frozen soil shrinks when it melts. This causes soil subsidence and erosion in a process that is largely irreversible. Once thermokarsting occurs, the phenomenon makes it difficult for vegetation to become reestablished.

Pika

Where should you walk in arctic tundra? Perhaps the best route is along streambeds. Since water isn't easily absorbed into tundra soil, even small amounts of rain can cause severe flooding of natural drainages. This flooding rips out any vegetation and leaves gravel and boulders in its place. Along these bouldery streambeds, boots do little damage to either soil or plants. If travel on vegetated tundra is unavoidable, choose ground that is dry, covered with grasses or sedges, and with few low shrubs or lichens. As elsewhere, spread out to minimize trampling damage.

Arctic Camping. Choosing a campsite in arctic tundra can be difficult. Since dry sites are scarce and damage takes so long to heal, select campsites with care. Botanist David Cooper found that four visitors camping for ten days on a lichen-rich community in Alaska's Brooks Range created a disturbed spot of more than twelve square yards. The disturbance eroded the lichen to bare mineral soil. Cooper suggests that recovery will take more than seventy-five years because the Brooks Range combines high altitude with high latitude, so growing conditions are especially harsh.

In arctic tundra, the best and often easiest travel routes are along gravel streams subject to periodic flooding.

The best campsites, therefore, are those that cause the least disturbance to soils and vegetation. They shouldn't be located in or near lichen-dominated stands, nor should they be situated in plant communities subject to thermokarsting. The edges of gravel streambeds make excellent campsites as long as you're aware that flash flooding is a possibility. Camping in the wide valleys found along many arctic streams makes you more visible to other travelers, so keep your camp out of sight if possible, and remember that sounds carry farther in a landscape where trees are few or nonexistent.

When streambeds are unavailable, look for mineral soil sites on mildly sloping land. On many tundra slopes, soil slippage is a common occurrence. You can often find a campsite just below these lobes of creeping soil. In a few years, the slow-moving earth will remove all traces of impact.

Arctic Sanitation. If you guessed that surface disposal is a viable method for much of the arctic environment, you are correct. Most areas see few visitors, and the long hours of summer sun, coupled with the alternative of damage to tundra vegetation, make surface deposition a reasonable choice.

In most areas where contact by others is likely, use a cathole, preferably in unfrozen, organic soil where damage to vegetation is minimal. However, any disposal method that 1) diminishes human, animal, and insect contact; 2) encourages decomposition; and 3) protects water quality is the best option. This is almost always going to be the cathole method. The best cathole sites in arctic environments are unfrozen, organic soils where damage to vegetation is minimal. You can often dig up a flap of sod, do your business, and then cover it to prevent direct contact with animals, insects, and precipitation.

Stonecrop

SUMMARY

Travel and Camp on Durable Surfaces

- Alpine and arctic vegetation can be extremely vulnerable to trampling. Because of slow growth rates, tundra recovers slowly from disturbance. Campsites should be located on rock, snow, or exposed mineral soil to avoid damaging vegetation.
- Gravel bars in drainages make ideal campsites if there is no danger of flash flooding.
- If you must camp on vegetated surfaces, place kitchens and packs on rocks or snow, spread tents out, and move camp often.
- To avoid undue trampling, stick to established trails or nonvegetated surfaces.

- If you choose to travel cross-country, spread out and walk on rock, snow, streambeds, or dry meadows.

Dispose of Waste Properly
- Catholes are the better option in waste disposal. Others may opt to carry out their waste.

Minimize Campfire Impacts
- Because of low forest productivity at and above timberline, fires are inappropriate. Bring and use a stove when traveling in alpine or arctic tundra.

10

Snow and Ice

Places with short growing seasons generally recover slowly once they are damaged, and except in the desert, the length of the growing season is largely determined by how long temperatures are below freezing. When the period of cold temperatures is relatively short, the land can quickly recover from mild disturbance. As the period of cold lengthens, the scars of impact become increasingly difficult to conceal. Although cold temperatures shorten the growing season, making recovery periods lengthy, cold can also make the land more durable by providing it with a protective coating of snow.

It's difficult to speak of cold without mentioning snow. For whenever the mercury in a thermometer begins to plunge and storm clouds gather, precipitation in the form of snow is usually not far behind. It may fall on us during summer high on a mountain glacier, or in winter while skiing through a forest. So the cold that makes the land less resilient once damage occurs also brings snow, which makes the land more resistant to damage in the first place.

Winter Travel

For a growing number of experienced backcountry visitors, winter is a special time. A wilderness that is noisy and crowded in summer becomes quiet and empty once snow falls. This, along with the rapid growth of cross-country skiing, may be why winter wildland use is growing in popularity. In Great Smoky Mountains National Park, Bill Hammitt and his coworkers found that winter visitors actually prefer winter trips over summer ones; most mentioned solitude and experiencing the winter environment as major reasons for this preference. They tended to avoid backpacking during summer because of heavy use by other visitors. Another interesting finding in this study was that winter visitors are often old hands, averaging at least ten years of backpacking experience. From such studies, we may conclude that as people become expert in the ways of wildlands, they'll find traveling the backcountry in winter even more appealing.

This shift in use is already occurring. In the national parks, winter visitation has increased 27 percent in the past decade; summer visitation has increased only 7 percent. At Yellowstone National Park, for example, winter use has grown so rapidly that managers are seriously talking about establishing visitor limitations.

Many of the traditional concerns about the impacts of summer travel are of little concern in winter. The number of visitors is low, and vegetation and soil are protected under a thick mantle of snow. Because so few visitors are present, it's not as crucial to maintain a low profile. Brighter-colored clothes and equipment aren't likely to be a visual impact on others and may even be desirable from a safety standpoint. There's also little concern over whether travel is along established routes or far from existing trails; most effects will be hidden by the next snowfall or the spring melt.

So what are our concerns in winter? Probably the most important is wildlife disturbance. In certain instances, such as when species desert an area entirely, wildlife disturbance is much more significant than are the obvious but highly localized impacts to vegetation and soil that occur along trails, campsites, and other areas of frequent use. If we lose the animals from wilderness ecosystems, we'll lose a critical part of what makes wilderness so valuable in the first place.

NOLS

Disturbance during winter affects animals at a time when they are particularly susceptible to stress; thus it's important to maintain a critical distance.

Like humans, wildlife find winter a particularly challenging and stressful season. Unlike humans, however, animals don't have sleeping bags to ward off the cold. They must somehow find food and shelter under deep snow or in windswept areas. And large animals can't travel on top of snow; they have to plow through it, using tremendous stores of energy when they cover long distances. Most animals employ a strategy of energy conservation: they limit their energy needs by minimizing their activities, including searching for food and escaping dangers. Clearly, this strategy is upset when animals are disturbed by recreationists. Flight or fright (both of which are associated with an increased heart rate) increases energy consumption, and the need for more food quickly arises. Acquiring this food often involves searching and traveling—activities that further drain energy—and can institute a vicious cycle of increased demand and stress. Although this may not be a serious problem for a healthy animal in a normal winter, it can be fatal for animals that are pushing the carrying capacity of their ranges or struggling through harsh winters.

To avoid such unnecessary disturbance to wildlife during winter, don't approach animals closely. Safe approach distance varies among species, among individuals within those species, and with local circumstances. This makes it difficult to develop a single rule of thumb about how close you can get to animals in winter. In Yellowstone National Park, elk that infrequently encountered people typically began to move when skiers came within 400 yards of them, but some moved when skiers were still a mile away, and others let skiers get as close as 125 yards. Perhaps the best guideline is to retreat when you can tell that the animal is aware of you. At this point, its heart rate is probably elevated and its energy expenditure increased. Use your best judgment, and remember that it can be all too easy to approach an animal too closely when you are on skis.

When selecting a campsite in the winter, try to avoid places that are used for feeding, watering, or sleeping. Animal sign is easy to detect when there is snow on the ground; look for tracks, bedding spots, and open water. If you see an abundance of sign, place your camp elsewhere.

Several studies show that animals are as likely to be upset by one person traveling alone as by a large group of people traveling together. This suggests that disturbance should be less if a large group stays together; fewer wildlife-human encounters occur with one large group than with many small ones. When encounters with other people in winter are unlikely, keeping a group together is preferable to dispersal. The most valid reasons for traveling in small groups are to minimize disturbance to other visitors and to avoid damaging off-trail areas, both of which are of relatively little concern in winter.

Early- and Late-Winter Concerns

Although a thick snow cover effectively protects underlying vegetation and soil from trampling, a thin and patchy cover renders it unusually vulnerable. When a thin blanket of snow is compressed and compacted, melting is delayed, shortening the growing season for plants. Even greater impact occurs where snow-free soils, saturated with meltwater from receding snowbanks, are trampled. Such soils become muddy quagmires of churned-up earth. Plants pressed into mud have little chance of survival, and plants growing in wet soils are easily uprooted by a sliding boot.

Summer concerns of trampling and concentrated use are absent during winter when snow provides a resistant surface. Most important is to select a site where the risk of water pollution is minimal.

Winter snow structures are appropriate . . .

Avoid backcountry travel during the snowmelt season, or visit either higher or lower elevations. This is particularly important for groups traveling with stock, given the potential for damage of a horse's hooves. If this isn't feasible, travel in small groups. Visit either remote places, where your disturbance won't be compounded by others following in your footsteps, or high-impact places that have already been disturbed. This latter option has its down side, however, in that damage to popular trails during snowmelt often makes costly repairs necessary.

Winter Camping
Because the impact of trampling is likely to be negligible on vegetation and soil covered by deep snow, many of the

WILL WATERMAN

. . . if they are dismantled after use.

camping techniques normally practiced in summer are unnecessary. Whether the site is pristine or well worn, there need be little concern for the resistance of the ground surface, the group size, length of stay, or location of tents, kitchens, and traffic routes. Most important is to select a site that will minimize the potential for wildlife disturbance and water pollution to dispose of human waste properly.

Any time you camp in snow, make some attempt to camouflage whatever disturbance you have created, unless snow is falling so fast that all evidence will soon be gone. If you build snow structures, dismantle them before you leave. This is very important in popular areas where others will soon follow. Although snow structures may be appreciated by other winter campers, leaving them intact runs counter to the

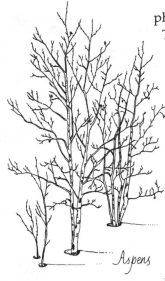

Aspens

philosophy of low-impact wilderness use. They provide a reminder that others have been there before, violate the principle of leaving areas as you found them, and may even be a safety hazard for others. The only exceptions to this guideline are when you plan to return to the site on the same trip or if you're in an area that is infrequently visited in winter.

Winter Sanitation

Proper disposal of human waste is difficult in a landscape covered with snow and ice. Feces typically can't be buried adequately because of deep snow or frozen ground. Cold temperatures and lack of intense sunlight retard the breakdown of fecal material. Therefore, in heavily used areas, packing out feces is usually the best alternative. This can be less unpleasant in winter, because once feces freeze, they are relatively odorless. Also, sleds are often available for hauling. In more remote and less used areas, feces decomposition is most rapid in direct sunlight; therefore, catholes just below the surface of the snow are acceptable, keeping in mind that your waste will be resting on the ground come spring.

Try to picture the drainage system in the area you are camping (this can be difficult given complete snow cover), and pick a site—such as a ridgetop—that's away from water and that nobody would choose to camp on. A thick grove of trees often makes a suitable waste site, not only because there is ample organic soil beneath the snow, but also because it guarantees that no one will choose such a site for a camp the following summer. Finally, because yellow snow creates an unpleasant visual impact, always cover urine stains with clean snow.

Winter Waste Concerns

Littering is often more of a problem in winter than in summer, especially in backcountry areas that experience heavy snowfall. Here, anything dropped into snow rapidly disappears until the following spring. In this respect, snow can give you a false feeling of security when you look around your winter campsite and see no evidence of litter you may have inadvertently dropped. Particularly hard to see against a white background are transparent candy wrappers, ski-wax scrapings, plastic bags, and white toilet paper.

How can you minimize the potential for inadvertent littering? In the case of individually wrapped food items, such as pieces of candy, prepackaging is an easy solution. Remove the wrappers before your trip, and package like items together in a single plastic bag. Keeping track of these plastic bags presents the same problem, but there are fewer of them. Plastic bags used for food are usually transparent, rendering food identification easy but making the bags difficult to see against a backdrop of white snow. Until a manufacturer produces a translucent colored bag that shows up against snow, winter visitors should be especially mindful of this litter potential.

If clear plastic is difficult to see in winter, white toilet paper is even harder. Consequently, some winter visitors take only paper of a dark color that contrasts with the snow. Toilet paper is difficult to burn in snow. Even when the surrounding snow is cold and dry, the snow soon melts, soaking the edges of the paper and leaving some unburned pieces. The easiest solution is to avoid using toilet paper. Snow—compressed and formed into a compact, oblong shape—provides a sanitary and surprisingly comfortable alternative. Best of all, when the snow melts, no evidence remains. Alternatively, pack the toilet paper out.

If snow is the only nearby source of water, concentrate cooking wastewater in a sump hole.

WILL WATERMAN

Dental floss and ski and candle wax are small but increasingly common litter problems in winter. Like plastic bags, they're highly visible come summer and not rapidly biodegradable. Consider using colored floss and candles; they won't be so easily lost in the snow. Stash ski wax scrapings in a plastic bag, and pack them out.

In most winter-camping situations, wastewater is not a problem. It's usually too cold to bathe, and often water is scarce, the only source being melting snow on a stove. Any leftover water you may have is from cooking. Scatter this excess wastewater wherever the ground is bare of snow. When surrounding snow is the only source of water, or if others may discover your camp before the next snowfall, concentrate the wastewater in a sump hole, well away from water sources.

As in other seasons, if your cooking results in extra food, pack it out. This is particularly true of leftover grease. Rather than discarding it in the snow to be found by animals, let it cool to a solid, bag it, and carry it out with your trash.

Winter Fires

There are several compelling reasons for not building fires in winter. Dead and down wood that is dry is essentially nonexistent, so the temptation is to tear off lower tree branches or to pull wood off standing snags. Moreover, it is extremely difficult to properly dispose of the remains of a fire built in snow. Therefore, fires aren't normally recommended except in emergencies. A somewhat less rigid but still acceptable policy acknowledges that although usually undesirable, fires aren't likely to cause damage if they're built infrequently, kept small, and confined to remote places seldom visited during any season. Don't disfigure trees when collecting firewood, and burn all wood down to ash.

Permanent Snow and Ice

If you travel far enough toward the polar regions or high enough in some mountain ranges, you will enter the realm of

SCOTT KANE

Visitors to permanent snow and ice, though often the most experienced in outdoor skills, haven't always practiced the best conservation techniques.

perpetual snow and ice. Here, snow has accumulated for millennia; moisture has been squeezed and compressed by the weight of each year's snowfall until most of the air is removed and all that remains below the surface snow is blue ice. Where snowfall has been great and much time has elapsed, the ice can be extremely thick. Into this hostile environment, where seasons are marked only by more or less snow accumulation, come humans. These areas, where winter never ends, are not as popular or as accessible as more temperate wildlands. Nonetheless, people have left their mark on the land.

If winter visitors generally exhibit higher levels of backcountry skills than do most summer visitors, those traveling to the extremes of snow and ice are often the most experienced of all. Indeed, at this edge of one of the earth's

most pristine yet harsh environments, the price of not knowing what you're doing may be your life.

Unfortunately, the most skilled people don't always practice the best conservation techniques. For if pristine wildlands are defined as places where evidence of people is
mostly lacking, then many of the more popular high-altitude
environments of snow and ice fall far short. One need only to
look at the vast amounts of trash and
garbage past expeditions have left on
Everest, Rainier, and Mount McKin-
ley. Discarding nearly everything in
their pursuit of the summit, large expeditions have littered their way up and down
many otherwise pristine mountains. In this environment, where extreme cold tends to preserve
everything, including human bodies, the only
excuse these users can provide is that snow
Snowshoe Hare will eventually cover their litter. The larger
question—like living with the knowledge
that there are golf balls lying on the surface of the moon—is
whether we have a responsibility to keep these pristine wildlands free from our material excesses.

How do we limit impact in these lands of snow and ice?
Because litter is such a problem, we can start by carrying out
everything we carry in—spent fuel cans, fixed ropes, tents,
extra food, even bamboo wands used to mark climbing
routes. Burying trash in the snow or dropping it into a crevasse is generally not acceptable, although it is practiced and
sometimes condoned in extreme cases such as high, ice-
locked peaks. In some cases, trash discarded into a "bottom-
less" crevasse early in the climbing season has floated to the
surface later in the summer, when melting water from a glacier rises to the surface.

Although more and more small expeditions, carrying
lightweight gear, conscientiously strive to practice litter
removal, one area where they often fall short is in route

marking. Fluorescent orange survey tape is commonly tied to the tops of bamboo wands and left to mark paths up and down the mountain. When the winds rise, scraps of this tape blow across snowfields and glaciers. Instead of flimsy survey tape, use red or orange duct tape on the wands. Properly secured, it won't blow away.

Other than litter, there are few impact problems related to travel and camping on permanent snow and ice. Campfires are not possible, and wildlife is practically nonexistent. The only remaining issue is sanitation; here, the challenge is body waste left in this extremely cold environment.

As in winter camping, packing out waste is best in popular areas, or a shallow snow cathole is entirely appropriate in remote areas or on little-used routes. Another acceptable disposal method in some places is to use crevasses. (Check local restrictions and recommendations.) Unlike trash and litter, which may float if the crevasse fills with water, solid human waste remains at the bottom of the ice. Although little is known about this practice, it is probable that the action of ice eventually moves the fecal waste to a lower elevation, where decomposition or dissipation occurs.

On popular snow and ice climbs without suitable crevasses, latrines have a special function. The concentration of human body waste, which we suggested you avoid in more temperate climates, is more acceptable in this cold environment where we can't expect feces to decompose. Here it's better to place a group's body waste in one location than to spread it over a large area, where the chance of others finding it is more likely and the potential for contamination of snow-melted water is increased. Latrines also provide privacy for members of a group. In contrast, scattered catholes and surface deposition offer none. As always, sanita-

Moose

tion problems can be reduced by traveling and camping in less-popular places and with smaller groups.

SUMMARY

Respect Wildlife
- Wildlife disturbances are the most critical concern of winter camping and traveling.
- Don't approach animals too closely, and keep your group together so that the animals will not be stressed by repeated encounters with dispersed groups of people.
- Camp away from places that are used during the winter for feeding, watering, or sleeping.

Travel and Camp on Durable Surfaces
- In the winter, when a protective covering of snow overlays vegetation and soil, most impact concerns are minimal.
- Vegetation is unusually vulnerable to damage when the snow cover is thin or patchy, however. Avoid use of the backcountry during the snowmelt season.
- If you build snow structures, dismantle them when you leave camp so that others will find the area unaltered by humans.

Dispose of Waste Properly
- Packing out feces is the best solution to winter waste disposal in heavily used areas. In remote areas, bury feces in catholes just below the surface of the snow.
- Try to picture the drainage system in the area, and avoid potential drainages for your cathole or surface deposition.
- Cover urine stains with clean snow.

- On glaciers, some areas require special methods of feces disposal; others recommend depositing human waste in crevasses or in latrines. Check with the land managers about specific regulations.
- Beware that trash is quickly covered by snow and can be lost only to reappear in the spring. Minimize the amount of potential trash by getting rid of excess packaging before you go into the backcountry.

If a Koyukon Indian wrote a book about bears, maybe half the volume would be the rules of keeping yourself in a state of respect toward the animal.

—Richard Nelson, Alaska anthropologist

11

Bear Country

It's a beautiful summer morning in the most pristine back-country in North America, with rugged snow-capped peaks, broad forested valleys, and meadows filled with elk and deer. You are hiking down a trail. Suddenly you stop. In the trail lies a pile of mashed berries, enough to fill a bucket. The pile still steams in the cool morning air. You think about it for a moment. Slowly the hair on the back of your neck rises and your heart climbs into your throat. Bears!

We may fear them or love them, but above all, we who visit the backcountry respect their power. For the bear is the world's largest land carnivore and one of the few animals that prey on humans. We don't seem able to make up our minds about bears: we have difficulty living close to them, yet most of us don't want to live without them, at least in remote wildland areas. The truth is, this animal that stirs up so many ambivalent feelings among backcountry users is more than just another wilderness species; for many, the bear is the symbol of truly wild country.

If a wilderness species means one that requires large amounts of relatively pristine habitat yet possesses a limited tolerance for humans in its wild state, then bears easily qual-ify. Here is an animal, like elk or moose, that generally does best in the absence of people. As the human presence grows, however, some animals lose their shyness and become habituated to human ways. When this happens, scientists say a species is "behaviorally corruptible."

Unlike the less aggressive elk or deer, once a bear becomes habituated, people won't tolerate its close company. When bears have lost their fear and interact freely with humans, there is danger—not just to humans, but also to bears. In the words of bear biologist Chris Servheen, perhaps a sharper definition of a true wilderness species might be an animal that best lives outside a human-influenced environment and that people refuse to tolerate in close association. If you apply this definition in light of the growing number of recreationists visiting bear country, it's obvious that bears may have more to fear from us than we do from them.

When Bear Meets Man

There are three recognized species of bears in North America: black, brown, and polar. Because polar bears inhabit country that is less accessible to most visitors, the following discussion applies mainly to black and brown bears; more specifically, to the brown bear subspecies considered most controversial: the grizzly. Although our primary concern is how to reduce impact on bears, a knowledge of the different evolutionary paths of bears helps in understanding their behavior when confronted by humans.

The black bear evolved in mountains and forests—areas with plenty of cover and trees. According to Stephen Herrero, author of *Bear Attacks*, when placed in a threatening situation, black bears usually flee or climb a tree instead of attacking. Still, between 1960 and 1980, black bears injured more than five hundred people in North America. Some 90 percent of these recorded bear-inflicted injuries were considered minor, however.

Grizzly and polar bears evolved in high plains and open meadows, tundra, and polar ice, with virtually no place to hide. Their best defense became a good offense, and herein lies the problem: they are unpredictably aggressive.

LURAY PARKER

The possibility of changing a bear's behavior once it has learned to exploit human food is remote.

Compared with black bears, grizzlies at first appear relatively benign. Herrero reports that grizzly bear attacks accounted for fewer than two hundred documented injuries between 1900 and 1980. Why is this number so low if grizzlies are much more aggressive than blacks? First, most wildland recreation takes place in country that is primarily black bear habitat. Second, black bears outnumber grizzlies by more than ten to one, so the chances of encountering a black bear are much greater. Although this may explain the comparatively smaller number of grizzly attacks, it tells us nothing about the severity of grizzly-inflicted injury. Nearly 50 percent of the injuries were classed as major, requiring hospitalization for more than twenty-four hours or resulting in death.

Aggressive bear encounters occur for a variety of reasons. Perhaps the most common are when a bear is surprised at close range, a female bear is protecting her young, or a bear is protecting a food source. In each of these instances, bears are defending what they deem is rightfully theirs, whether it be space, young, or food. Far less common in wild populations, but more frequent where they've become habituated to humans, are bears that actively pursue people as prey.

Although their life histories, habitats, and responses to people vary considerably, the three bear species have several basic traits in common: they are long-lived, intelligent, and opportunistic. Because bears have the ability to take advantage of any food source within their environment, once they have exploited human food, they continue to seek it out. The possibility of changing their behavior after bears have received such positive reinforcement is remote. Before 1970, more than half of all grizzly-inflicted injuries in national parks occurred in Yellowstone National Park, where bears had become "corrupted" by feeding at garbage dumps and campgrounds.

Black Bear

From this brief survey of bear behavior, we might conclude that all bears are dangerous and that encounters between bears and people can and do lead to serious injury. There is another side to the coin, however: human-caused injury to bears. When people invade their habitat and conflict occurs, bears are heavy losers. Since the settlement of the contiguous United States, the grizzly's population has dwindled from an estimated one hundred thousand bears to probably fewer than one thousand. When conflict results in injury to people, the bear is often destroyed. During the twentieth century, grizzlies were responsible for less than twenty human deaths in the lower forty-eight states. Since 1968, several hundred grizzlies have been killed—most close to or within the boundaries of national parks—because they were considered a threat to human life or property. Both bears and people have much to gain by mutual avoidance.

Bear Avoidance

The easiest way to avoid bears is to stay away from those wildland areas where bears live. For visitors who fear bears or who fear for bears, this choice is sound and, in specific instances, may have strong merit. This option, however, limits backcountry use to relatively few areas, since bears—particularly black bears—inhabit such a large and varied amount of wildland that a map of their range covers most of North America. Assuming that most visitors want to enjoy lands where bears still roam, the next best choice is to avoid a confrontation. If your actions are successful, you will see no bears or, at most, a distant one.

Once you've made a commitment to avoid bears, you need to know the species of bear you're trying to avoid. Perhaps even more important, learn whether the area has a history of bear-people conflict. Get information from the land-managing agency, as well as from others who have visited the area. Then evaluate the potential for a possible encounter, choosing a level of avoidance that lessens your chances of confrontation. Hiking the Appalachian Trail in the Great Smokies, where you may expect black bears to be habituated to human food, requires a level of precaution that you may choose to ignore in Colorado, where black bears are normally aloof and secretive. The level of avoidance should grow in relation to the potential for conflict; backpacking Alaska's coastal tundra, where you may encounter both polar bears and grizzlies, calls for the highest level of bear-avoidance techniques.

In the following discussion, we assume a worst-case scenario. You're in backcountry that harbors bears habituated to humans, or you fear that an encounter may produce some unpleasant results (to you or to the bear), or both. Sometimes our recommendations in this circumstance run counter to practices we advocate in situations where bears are absent or where conflicts with humans are rare. A careful judgment must be made when concern for your safety or the safety of bears outweighs your goal of minimizing impact to other aspects of the wildland environment. Weigh all of the factors—bear species, the potential for conflict, and the possible consequences of that conflict—then choose the technique that best reduces your chance of an encounter and at the same time harms the backcountry the least.

There are three general guidelines to lessen the chance of a bear encounter. First, do everything you can to avoid surprising a bear. All bears have a critical space they will defend if they feel threatened. This space varies with environment, time of year, abundance of food, and the individual bear. The critical distance may be as little as a few feet for a black bear, 150 feet for a male grizzly, or as much as several hundred yards for a grizzly sow with cubs. If you're far enough away that a bear doesn't consider you a threat, then your chances for avoiding a confrontation are good. Usually, when a bear gets a whiff of human scent or hears human noise, and is not confronted within its critical space, it quickly leaves.

Polar Bear

Second, should you find yourself accidentally inside a bear's critical space, maximize your presence. If challenged with what it perceives as a threat, a bear will size it up and act accordingly. At some point, a bear will flee and not confront the danger; this decision appears to depend at least partially on the physical size of the threat. For black bears, one person may elicit a bear's fast retreat; for grizzlies, the more people, the better. Statistics on grizzly attacks show that large groups of people are safer than small ones. There are no documented attacks on parties of six or more, and your chances are extremely good even with a group of four people. For this reason, if you travel in grizzly country, your group should be large enough to ensure some measure of safety.

Finally, avoid attracting bears. A bear's sense of smell is excellent; they're attracted by food smells and other odorous materials, such as fish, soap, and deodorant. Make every effort to reduce these bear-attracting odors to a minimum, and keep them apart from your sleeping area.

Traveling in Bear Country

You can minimize the chance of a confrontation in bear country by avoiding certain seasons and by planning your route away from specific places where bears are most likely to be found. Bears usually travel far and wide in search of food, and depending on the season, you can make some general assumptions about their presence in relation to food sources. During spring, after a winter of inactivity, a bear often feeds on young vegetation on lower southern exposures, the first ground opened to the sun. In summer, a bear may range from the seashore to above timberline, living up to its reputation as a wandering omnivore and feasting on everything from dead whales to alpine flowers. Come autumn, abundant berry patches and fish-spawning streams are favorite bear habitat. Often, simply using areas other than these will lessen your chances of encountering a bear. But what do you do if you find yourself unavoidably in prime bear habitat?

Like people, bears usually choose familiar paths of least resistance. Stay away from game trails through brush or forest, particularly bear trails found along spawning streams, rivers, and berry patches, and through passes on ridgetops. These trails often consist of staggered oval depressions, as bears commonly step in the same places, or they may be two distinct lanes, the distance apart of a bear's legs. Don't camp near such trails or close to human trails, as bears use these too, especially at night.

As you travel in bear country, be conscious of tracks, scat, and mounds of excavated earth where a bear has dug for food. Consider traveling out of the area and camping elsewhere if you see an abundance of these signs. Avoid all carrion or places with the smell of decaying meat; you may be near a bear's food cache. After eating their fill, bears—particularly grizzlies—often cover a kill with dirt, branches, or forest litter, and then bed close by. If a grizzly is near its food cache, it will be short-tempered and unpredictable. Stop as soon as you smell something foul, and give it a wide berth.

In grizzly country, hiking groups of four or more people are statistically safer than smaller groups. Since few grizzly attacks have occurred where people are gathered close together in numbers of four or more, we must assume that there's some imposing feature in a group's appearance that deters grizzlies from an aggressive response, even when their critical space is violated. Nonetheless, a group is ineffective if its members are not close together.

Making loud noises along the trail is another way to ensure that you don't surprise a bear. Whistling, singing, ringing a bell, clapping, and loud talking are all effective. This should be done any time a group enters a forest, brushy area, willow patch, or terrain where visibility is impaired, such as rolling hills or dips in tundra. Never make noises like a hurt animal or a bear, since these sounds may act as an attractant. Keep in mind that roaring streams mask sounds, so be particularly cautious when approaching one without an open view. Finally, it's best to leave your dog at home. Most dogs bark at a bear; then when the bear chases the dog, it attempts to hide behind its owner.

Campsite Selection

When choosing a campsite in bear country, keep away from places where bears are commonly found—their food sources and travel paths. Usually, the best choice is to select an elevated campsite in moderately open country. This practice allows both you and a bear greater chance of detection and less chance for surprise.

Where you anticipate bears, especially grizzlies, your kitchen site should determine your campsite. Here it's best to forgo the normal practice of keeping all food far from water. Locating the kitchen close to running water helps keep the area free of food odors by absorbing and transporting minute food particles and cooking wastewater away from your

In bear country, locate your camp in moderately open country where approaching bears may readily be seen, but with a scattering of possible escape trees. Locate the cooking site a minimum of one hundred yards downwind of tents, preferably near water to carry away odors. Suspend food from trees near the cooking site or store on the ground at least one hundred yards from both your tent and the cooking site. Leave your pack outside the tent with flaps open.

campsite. Designate one general cooking area for the group by a stream, then position the sleeping area at least one hundred yards from this site. If the terrain allows, locating tents out of the streambed and up on a bluff will keep food odors away from the sleeping area.

If camping along the streambed is the only possibility, choose a site at least one hundred yards upstream of the cooking area. The usual down-valley winds of the evening will keep food odors from the sleeping area most nights. It's true that up-valley winds of the morning may reverse the process and blow odors in your direction; if a confrontation occurs, however, it's far better if it happens during daylight, when the bear is easily seen.

In brushy or flat lowland areas, the camping choices are less clear. Here you should keep to more open areas and maintain at least the one-hundred-yard minimum distance from your cooking site.

If you're camping along the coast, camp on the beach instead of in the nearby forest. Out in the open, you will have a better chance of forming a group if you're confronted by a bear. Cook close to the high-tide line, then sleep at least one hundred yards up or down the beach from this area.

In-Camp Techniques

After setting up camp, practice impeccable camping by keeping all food and food odors separated from your sleeping area. Plan your meals so that what is cooked is promptly eaten. Don't spill food or wipe your hands or utensils on your clothes. The smells of fish and of greasy foods are especially attractive to a bear; minimize their contact with clothing and equipment. Consider cooking in special clothing, such as nylon wind gear, that you leave at the cooking site and that can be easily washed. Many people even wear a stocking hat over their hair, since hair readily absorbs food odors. After each meal, wash your face and hands in the stream.

Place all food and cooking gear in specified bags, minimize food contact with the rest of your equipment, and keep odorous articles like soap and toothpaste in the cooking area. Remember to transfer trail food from daypacks back to cooking sites by nightfall. Under no circumstances keep food of any kind in your tent.

If you've located your cooking site beside a stream, clean utensils of all food particles, rinse them directly in the stream, then bag them with your remaining food. Any minor food residue will be washed downstream. Small amounts of cooking water can also be deposited in the stream rather than scattered widely, as is normally recommended. Use your best judgment as you evaluate the volume

Kinnikinnick

and resiliency of the stream. High-volume rivers or streams can withstand direct immersion when you are washing pots; low-volume streams, on the other hand, simply can't absorb this kind of impact. If you choose not to use this method because of possible pollution of the stream, use a sump—a shallow hole in organic soil—in order to concentrate wastewater in one spot and minimize the spread of odors. Always cover this hole with sand or soil after use.

If you carry canned meat, cook and eat it just before leaving camp. Burn the can in a fire to destroy the odor, then place it in a plastic bag and carry it out. Any knife used to clean fish should be kept with other cooking articles, and the fish themselves should be cooked and eaten immediately; don't save them for breakfast. It's best to catch fish away from camp and clean them there. Use the same discretion as in deposition of wastewater. If the stream has an ample volume and the area is used infrequently, throw the viscera back into the water to be carried downstream. If the stream is too small to absorb this kind of impact, or if the area is subject to more than occasional use, deposit the fish remains at least a quarter mile from camp.

Around camp, always be cautious of bears, even though there may be no evidence indicating their presence. Most experts agree that it's advisable to sleep in tents in bear country. Although a tent is no protection against a determined bear, it may dissuade a mildly curious one from approaching closer. If you still desire to sleep under the stars, you should always be near a tent, ready to get inside if a bear is suspected in the area. The first person rising in the morning must be particularly alert and should walk to the cooking area with appropriate noise and a visual check of the area.

If you wander away from camp when scouting for firewood or to relieve yourself, be extra cautious in grizzly habitat. An excursion near camp is probably safe because of the noise from camp activities, but a longer walk is best made with a minimum of four people.

Protecting Your Food

Losing food to a bear creates problems for both bears and visitors. The bear becomes habituated to obtaining food from humans, making it almost certain that a confrontation will eventually occur. Moreover, you may have to cut short your trip because your food, and perhaps your equipment, is gone. In remote areas where access is limited, your survival may depend on these items. Thus it's particularly important to store them in a location that is as bear-resistant as you can make it.

Hanging food high and close to the trunk of a tree usually suffices in grizzly country, but not where black bears are a problem.

Keep your food at least one hundred yards from your tent site. In forest or dense brush, the safest storage area is often your cooking area. Food odors are concentrated in one location, and no one risks a trip to yet another place to gather or retrieve the food containers.

Where trees are common, visitors often hang their food out of reach of bears. But if bears are long habituated to humans, securing food from experienced bear "thieves" can prove challenging, to say the least. Where bears are particularly adept, sometimes the managing agency provides a method of protecting food. You should realize, however, that established storage facilities may be indicative of an area with "problem" bears, and even these methods may not suffice against a determined animal.

Numerous methods of food hanging have been devised, from simple poles that lift a container of food high up the trunk of a tree to elaborate suspension systems hung between two or more trees. Your choice of methods often depends on the ease of construction and the bear species. (Unlike black bears, adult grizzlies aren't usually adept climbers, but their reach is great; young grizzlies are often agile climbers.) Rigging a suspension system each night is a laborious task, but it

To suspend your food, use about one hundred feet of eighth-inch or larger nylon rope.

BEAR ATTACKS, THE LYONS PRESS

must be done correctly if you want to protect your food. Get into a routine every day, whether or not fresh bear sign is evident. Always allow ample time at the end of the day not only to cook, but also to hang your food before darkness falls. The best intentions most often fail when you arrive late in camp and don't properly protect your food.

In bear habitat without trees, food protection isn't as simple. Usually, open country means you're more likely to encounter grizzlies, but often these bears are less habituated to human presence and aren't expecting a handout. Store your food on the ground (wrapping it in extra plastic bags may reduce odors) at least one hundred yards from your tent site and cooking area. If you place your food bags in separate locations, chances are even better a bear won't discover all the food in one night. It's wise to mix your meals so that all breakfasts or suppers aren't

Grizzly Bear   in the same food bag; then if a bear discovers a bag, you won't lose all of one kind of food. Although this method is not as foolproof as hanging, in open country there are few options. Above all, never sleep with food; it's better to lose your food than to risk a close encounter with a bear.

Recently, new products for protecting food have appeared that may make former methods obsolete. One is a bear-resistant, unbreakable plastic container. Rangers in Alaska's Denali National Park report excellent results when backpackers carry food in this lightweight container with a tight-fitting but removable end. From 1982 to 1987, incidence of bears obtaining food from backpackers dropped 74 percent. These bear-resistant containers are commercially available and are sometimes required by land management agencies. Another device is a lightweight, battery-operated electric shock fence that discourages bears from reaching food and other equipment placed inside. Preliminary tests at NOLS and elsewhere have been promising, particularly for groups that can afford the extra pounds. One thing we've learned the hard way—don't step out at night without knowing the fence location.

Sanitation in Bear Country

Like many other animals, bears search out and excavate what humans bury, including feces. For this reason, surface deposition is especially appropriate in bear country, provided all other factors (impact levels, water pollution, direct contact) are carefully considered. In popular areas that are also frequently used by bears, catholes may present the only realistic option; possible excavation by a bear is not sufficient reason to forgo burying feces if you suspect that other people may find your waste.

Menstruation may present a problem for women traveling where bears are common. Recently, in a Canadian laboratory, researcher Bruce Cushing tested polar bears for their attraction to seal scent (the odor of the natural prey of polar bears) and human menstrual blood. Both elicited a maximal response from captive bears. In later field tests, used tampons were detected by polar bears nearly two-thirds of the time. Although these tests are far from offering conclusive evidence that menstruating women are subject to attack by bears, it does suggest that women who are traveling and camping in bear country should use caution. Where black bears are the only kind of bear, the potential danger is much less. But perhaps in grizzly or polar bear country, the best precaution for women is to use tampons rather than pads.

Disposal of used tampons is a problem that is less easily solved. Burial almost guarantees excavation where bears are active, possibly habituating bears to the taste of human blood. Moreover, the usual practice of triple-bagging used tampons and packing them out with other trash isn't the best solution from the standpoint of safety. Perhaps the best compromise is to burn the tampons in a hot fire, making sure they're completely consumed. If not, bag up the charred remains and pack them out as trash; the odor will be gone and the danger much diminished.

A New Perspective

Travel into any wildland area always entails risk. Although the practices we've outlined may reduce your chances of a confrontation with a bear, they don't guarantee your safety. An element of risk will always be present, for very little is known for certain about bear behavior in relation to humankind. Like people, bears are intelligent, unpredictable, and capable of inflicting great harm; it is for these reasons that we respect them.

One thing seems certain, however: It's time we began thinking from the perspective of this wilderness species before its wildness disappears and we're left with an animal that no longer symbolizes wild country. It is people who have entered into the last strongholds of the bear, not the other way around. Our behavior must reflect our respect and protect bears from humans, as much as humans from bears.

SUMMARY

Respect Wildlife
- Avoid surprising bears by making noise when hiking.
- Hike in groups of four or more to deter grizzlies.
- Be aware of bear sign—scat, digs, trails, or carrion. Consider traveling out of the area if you see an abundance of such sign.

Campsite Selection
- Choose an elevated campsite in moderately open country so that both you and a bear can detect each other's presence.
- Locate your kitchen close to running water to keep the area free of food odors. Position the sleeping area at least one hundred yards upstream from the kitchen. If possible, locate the tents out of the streambed and up on a bluff to keep odors out of the sleeping site.

Plan Ahead and Prepare
- Once bears have exploited human food, they continue to seek it out. These "corrupted" bears often end up being destroyed, so bearproof food storage is critical for both human and bear safety.

- Clean utensils of all food particles, and rinse them directly into the stream. Small amounts of cooking water can also be deposited in the stream if it has enough volume. If not, dig a sump, deposit wastewater in the hole, and cover it with soil to reduce food odors.
- Place all food and cooking gear in specified bags, minimize food contact with the rest of your equipment, and keep odorous articles like soap and toothpaste with the food and out of the sleeping area.
- Food should be hung from trees or stored in bearproof containers.

Dispose of Waste Properly
- Bears seek out and excavate human feces; for this reason, surface deposition is especially appropriate in bear country, provided other factors (impact levels, water pollution, direct contact) are taken into consideration.

12

Horsepacking

Humans have been sharing their work loads with pack stock for hundreds of years. During this time, the variety of animals used for packing has been rivaled only by the ingenuity of packing methods.

Today it is most common for the backcountry traveler to use horses or mules, but packers also rely on other animal species to get the job done. Although most of the low-impact methods cited in this chapter deal with horses, mules, and burros, variations of these concepts can be applied to other pack stock.

More than seven hundred years ago, the warrior Genghis Khan used thousands of tough mountain ponies on a hit-and-run campaign across much of the then known world. Genghis Khan and his warriors packed and rode these horses on numerous raids, moving at a rapid pace through rugged country. The ability to load a horse with gear or loot, then move on quickly to the next conquest, was perfected by his warrior packers.

The horse found its way to the Western Hemisphere in 1519, when Hernando Cortés landed in what is now Mexico with six hundred men and a small herd of sixteen horses. The Spanish ventured far into the New World, traveling in rough country with pack stock.

During the next four hundred years, others followed, using saddle horses and pack animals, including mules and donkeys. Different methods of packing animals evolved as humanity's relationship with pack stock grew. Native Americans, the Spanish, and others all had direct influence on methods of packing stock. Some of these early methods are still used. In addition, other pack animals, most notably llamas and goats, have entered the scene (these animals, too, have a long history of use in other countries). In the backcountry of today, it is possible to meet backpackers, horsepackers, goat packers, and even dog packers, all on the same trail.

Reducing Impact

Any activity that we undertake in the backcountry can cause lasting damage, but the challenges facing the horsepacker intent on keeping impact to a minimum are particularly daunting. There are several reasons why it is more difficult for a stock party to minimize impact than for a backpacking party to do so. First, horses are simply heavier than people. A standing horse typically exerts ten to twenty times the static pressure of a standing person. Consequently, potential impact on soil and vegetation is greater. Second, stock typically graze, defoliating vegetation. Third, stock don't dispose of their waste in places that are out of sight and away from water sources. Fourth, horses need to be excluded from established campsites. This can create additional disturbance to places that would not be disturbed otherwise. Stock trample places that hikers don't, such as the sides of trails and stream crossings. They are more likely to bring in weeds through their manure. And finally, encounters with stock groups are generally more of an intrusion to others' sense of solitude than encounters with other hikers.

All of these reasons why stock groups can be particularly destructive can be mitigated by using extra caution. But stock parties need to be even more careful than backpackers when using minimum-impact techniques. Stock parties should also take advantage of several unique opportunities for being light on the land. They have more ability to carry heavy loads. They can carry out other people's trash, and they are better able to carry low-impact equipment such as fire pans, fire blankets, and bear-resistant food boxes.

Although minimum-impact horsepacking is highly challenging, it can also be highly rewarding. Rewards include participating in a traditional activity, companionship with a unique and versatile animal, and using the horse's size and abilities to help decrease impact to the land.

For any modern backcountry traveler, reduction is essential. This is also true in horsepacking, and for many years horsepackers have been practicing what are called the three *R*s:

1. Reduce the number of animals.
2. Reduce the duration of stay.
3. Reduce the level of confinement.

Following these three simple guidelines helps horsepackers keep impact to a minimum.

Reducing the Number of Animals. Large herds of equines, like large numbers of elk, cattle, and humans, have an impact on the land simply because concentrated use means concentrated damage. If you use fewer pack animals, however, impact can be kept low.

Also keep it light. There's a real temptation among people who haven't been around horses (and some who have) to overload them with heavy gear. Actually, a human can pack more weight in proportion to body size than a horse. Most veteran packers recommend about 150 pounds per horse. Use nylon tents instead of heavy wall tents. Reduce weight by taking light, dehydrated food, instead of the canned food that was favored by outfitters in the past, and efficient, portable stoves, like those used by backpackers. A pack horse, more than a riding horse, has an awkward work load. A rider can shift his weight around as a horse climbs the trail, but a pack horse is carrying immobile weight. Therefore, it is important to balance the load and try to keep it as comfortable as possible.

The weight reductions you make before you reach the trailhead help reduce the number of animals. For a two-week trip, one pack horse is sufficient for two people who use lightweight gear.

Reducing the Duration of Stay. Progressive travel, the practice of moving camp frequently, is becoming more and more favored by horsepackers. Many move their camps each day. This way, horses do not graze or trample the same spot. Camping impact, too, may be decreased by moving often.

Moreover, as horses are packed and ridden each day, they come into camp tired and ready to eat, and they are less likely to wander at night if they are busy eating.

Reducing the Level of Confinement at Camp. Many horsepackers agree that the more a horse is confined, the more it doesn't want to be. Horses are flight animals whose instincts are to flee rather than to fight. The less horses are confined, the lighter they are on the land, while close confinement at campsites can cause great impact.

There are many methods of restraining pack stock, and all have advantages and disadvantages. Used improperly, even the best method can cause damage. For large groups, one approach capitalizes on the animals' herding instinct. Restrain only the herd leader using a picket or a battery- or solar-powered electric fence, and then hobble or turn loose the less dominant animals, thereby spreading the impact of most of the animals over a greater area (see "Keeping Your Horses at Camp").

Plan Ahead and Prepare

Low-impact horsepacking is much like any other backcountry activity. Horses are a means of getting into the wilds, just like a backpacker's feet. In today's ever-changing and diverse recreational society, the equestrian might also be a backpacker, kayaker, or climber, and some of the techniques used for these activities can also be applied to horsepacking.

As with any other recreational pursuit, horsepacking calls for thoughtful preparation. NOLS founder Paul Petzoldt often said, "Prior planning prevents poor performance." This is true of horsepacking. Here are some tips:

- *Know your animal.* Horses that spook easily, resist confinement, wander off, bully other horses, and are generally difficult are not good choices to take into the backcountry. It's a good bet that if your horse is a handful in the pasture at home, he'll be a hellion in the hills. At the same time, however, there is no substitute for saddle and trail experience for a young horse. Many good horsemen like to take younger horses out on short trips in the mountains to get them used to the surroundings.
- *Work with your horse.* Traveling into the backcountry with an inexperienced horse is a little like wearing a new pair of hiking boots on a trip without breaking them in first. It's important to work with your horse at home in the pasture before taking it into the backcountry. If it has never been packed, pack it. If the horse has never been in a portable electric fence, try one out at home. If it has never been hobbled, practice in the pasture. Training in a corral or arena can also help accustom horses to obstacles they might see on the trail. Many horse clubs sponsor trail class events that feature deadfall, mazes, and small bridges, all in the safety of an arena. Try them out. Also ride your horse through streams before trying this feat in the backcountry.
- *Take the right gear.* Think of your horse's needs as well as your own. If you are traveling in the summer, take along equipment that is going to make your horse comfortable. A small daily portion of grain provides additional energy for working horses and reminds the horse that camp is home. Take along insect repellent if pests are particularly bothersome. Bring whatever restraint device you need to keep your horse close to camp.
- *Know the country.* Inquire about unfamiliar country at U.S. Forest Service, Bureau of Land Management,

National Park Service, or other agency offices. Ask about restrictions regarding horse use, and find out if there is adequate pasture at campsites. If an area is overused, think about going elsewhere. In some places, grazing is prohibited and packing in stock food is a necessity. Pellets or cubes are better than hay; grain should be rolled or crushed so that seeds don't have any chance of germinating. If you have to use hay—a practice that is illegal in some areas of the country— make sure it is certified weed-free, a requirement on many federal lands. Feed your horses weed-free hay for several days before the trip to avoid dispersing noxious weed seeds in their manure.

On-Trail and Off-Trail Travel

Keep your animals in single file on a trail. Horses in a long pack string can be difficult to control, but try to keep the animals in line moving along the trail. Faster horses should lead the string so that they don't crowd or try to pass the slower ones. If you need to adjust a load, look for narrow spots where horses are confined and their movement restricted.

If you decide to go off-trail, try not to use paths that are starting to show signs of impact. Disperse your impact in areas where there are no signs of previous use. Let your stock travel abreast to avoid trampling vegetation and creating a path that others might be tempted to follow. Durable surfaces such as dry meadows or hard-packed ridges are good places for traveling single file. For trips with lots of off-trail travel, keep group size small and your stay short.

When you rest, choose a durable spot well off the trail. Hobble your horse and let it graze. Lightweight hobbles are available from many manufacturers and are ideal for temporary hobbling. Many horsepackers like to tie their horses to trees for short periods of time, although others feel that this is not a good practice. Damaging bark or roots is unacceptable, but if you feel you can tie a horse to a tree without these impacts, then it can be an effective method of restraint for a

When traveling on a trail, keep saddle and pack horses in single file.

short period of time. Large trees, eight inches or more in diameter, can withstand tying better than small trees. Wrap the rope around the trunk twice, and keep your rest stops short. By putting hobbles on your horse, you can prevent it from pawing the dirt around tree roots.

If you come across hikers or other horse users, look for a safe spot to pass. This may mean holding up your pack string. Hikers should move off the trail on the downhill side, because a spooked horse is easier to control uphill than down. Talk to any people you pass so that your horses recognize human voices. Sometimes backpacks scare horses. When passing, it is preferable to pass where you will create the least impact, such as on a dry meadow or gently sloping hillside. Llamas and horses are often intolerant of one another on the trail, so you will need to be especially watchful for these pack stock. Llama use is on the rise in public lands, and some

Off-trail travel with pack stock is best done over durable surfaces that can withstand impact.

horsepackers have even gone so far as to have llama enthusiasts bring their long-necked furry companions to horse pastures to habituate them. Horses and llamas eventually come to tolerate each other, for in South America they have worked side by side for hundreds of years.

Camping

Picking the Best Campsite.
As with backpacking, campsite selection is one of the keys to low-impact use. With stock, given their need for adequate feed and their high potential for impact when constrained, campsite selection is even more critical.

Stock impact can generally be minimized by visiting popular places and camping on well-worn sites in these popular areas. This has the advantage of confining use to places that are already so highly impacted that further use by conscientious stock parties should cause little additional impact. The disadvantage in choosing these sites is that horse feed may be hard to come by. This can be overcome by packing feed. Visiting popular places and camping on well-worn sites is particularly important if your group is large, if you plan a long stay, or if you aren't particularly skilled in minimum-impact camping.

If you are prepared to use extra caution, it is possible to visit remote places and camp on pristine sites without causing excessive impact. This will require more diligent campsite selection and more attention to stock confinement. Stays should be short—generally no more than one night per site. And restrained horses should be rotated frequently so that no impact occurs.

A campsite should be far enough off-trail to avoid conflicts with other recreationists, yet close enough to prevent pioneering new routes to the area. It should also have adequate feed and a good view of the pasture area in case your horses get into trouble during the night. When picking a camp, try to select one that has plenty of exposure to sunshine to help break down horse manure. Find a place where

When taking a rest break along the trail, it's far better to let horses graze randomly than to tie them to trees.

your horses don't need to be right in camp. Upon arriving, unload your pack and saddle stock quickly, and then attend to their needs.

The availability of feed probably determines the feasibility of a good campsite as much as anything. Look for areas that fit the type of restraint you might be using. For example, if trees and brush dominate the landscape, a picket might not be the best choice. Look for places with abundant forage and grass that has good seed heads and is not coarse or in a marsh. Be sure not to use an overgrazed area or overgraze an area that you use. If you use a picket or electric fence, you will need to move horses often. In Yellowstone National Park, one of the few national parks that allows horse grazing, rangers recommend that no more than a third of the annual forage be grazed by pack stock, leaving the remainder for wildlife.

Extended Camping. If you wish to stay in an area for an extended time, first ask yourself what the impacts of staying there for several nights would be. Is the area large enough to accommodate your horses? Will there be minimal impacts? Instead of camping several nights in one spot, consider progressive travel—moving both horses and camp several times during a lengthy stay. Even if you only move across a large meadow, you are spreading out use over a larger area, thus reducing concentrated impact.

In Camp. In camp, give your horses supplemental feed in nose bags or on a poncho or tarp to prevent the horses from digging into the soil to get every last morsel. Supplemental feed also reduces straying.

If you carry salt for your horses (probably not necessary on short trips up to two weeks), provide it in a container that will not allow salt to seep onto the ground, killing nearby vegetation.

When watering horses, choose a spot that is durable or is an obvious stream crossing. Look for spots where the banks are shallow, rocky, and able to withstand horse trampling. Recent research indicates that horses use streams and riparian zones for watering and some grazing but prefer grazing drier forage away from water. In a 1993 study of wild horses in Wyoming, researcher Crosby Allen found that the horses spent only 11 percent of their time in riparian zones and 85 percent on the uplands, far from water.

When breaking camp, scatter the horse manure, pack out all litter and excess feed or salt, and fill in or repair any holes created by the stock.

Keeping Your Horses at Camp. Once you find a camp that has pasturage, you must decide how to keep your horses where you want them. There are four options for handling your stock while they are grazing: hobbling, picketing, electric fencing, or loose herding. These can be used individually or in combination. They vary in their impact potential, their level of security, and their convenience.

Hobbling is one of the best ways to minimize impact. It works well in many cases, especially where horses are used to it and where there are few obstructions, such as in an open meadow. Hobbling horses is safer than leaving them loose, because you have a method of control. The disadvantage is that you don't have maximum control. Some hobbled horses can move almost as fast as unfettered ones. If this is the case, keep a herd boss picketed nearby so that your hobbled horses will not wander off.

Before hobbling, walk your horse to the area you wish grazed. Avoid obstacles such as big rocks or boulders, trees, and stumps. The ground should be covered with adequate feed but should not be in a marshy area where a horse can bog down. Remember that the horse's mobility is limited.

Placing bells on your horses is an excellent way to keep track of your hobbled or loose-herded horses. Horsepackers

When hobbling horses, pick a subordinate horse and turn it out on good grass, confining a dominant animal.

often learn to recognize the tones of different bells and thus can distinguish among horses just by sound.

Picketing horses is another popular method of restraint. The advantage of picketing is that it is an easy way to control your stock and allow them to graze. The disadvantage is that there is a high potential for overgrazing and concentrated trampling damage, particularly if pickets are not rotated frequently, and picketing is illegal in some areas. If you decide to use pickets, picket a minimum number of animals. It often works well to picket herd boss horses and let the others loose.

When choosing a picket site, avoid obstacles that will harm or impede the horse, such as brush, large rocks, and trees. Sufficient feed is especially important to picketed horses. From the center of the picket circle, walk its circumference, looking for anything that might hang up the rope and for the type of forage that will be within the horse's reach. Picketing with a soft rope will be a little easier on the land than a chain or coarse rope. It will also be easier on the horse if it gets tangled and starts to struggle. Picket the horse by a front foot, not by the halter. Many good horses picketed by the halter have been injured or even killed when they became tangled with the rope.

Move pickets repeatedly to avoid overgrazing, searching always for the best spot for your horse. This can mean moving pickets every few hours to avoid damage. The sensitivity of the meadow and abundance of forage will determine the frequency of rotation. Done correctly, picketing can cause relatively little impact. Done incorrectly, it can be one of the most abusive methods of restraint.

For many packers, especially those with larger groups containing more animals, picketing and hobbling in combination is the preferred method. A boss horse or an older mare is picketed on good grass (dense grass with good seed heads in a drier area), while the other horses are turned out with hobbles. The horses that are hobbled probably will not stray too far from the picketed horse, yet will move far enough to spread out impact. In large herds, sometimes two or even

Picketed horses should be moved often to avoid damage to the resource. A dominant horse is the best choice for picketing.

three horses are picketed, with the remainder hobbled. The picketed horses are moved often, but the hobbled horses move themselves. Remember to bell the hobbled horses.

Portable, battery- or solar-powered electric fences have revolutionized horse use in recent years because the fences are easy to erect, move, and take down. They probably provide the best combination of easy stock control and minimum impact, if used properly. They work well with stock that are accustomed to them. The fences, which can be purchased from tack and feed stores as well as a number of outfitting catalogs, use a thin wire or tape that conducts a small jolt of electricity. A horse that touches the wire soon learns to give it a wide berth. If you plan to use an electric fence, it is essential that you first familiarize your horses with this method before taking it into the backcountry. Electric fences will keep horses out of an area, and they can also be used to corral horses. If natural barriers exist on three sides of a potential pasture area, the fourth side can be fenced with the portable fence.

Raven

Although electric fences are easy to use and can be excellent for low-impact stock use, there are several disadvantages. First, as with other methods, the stock, and thus the fence, must be moved. Fences usually need not be moved as frequently as pickets; in some areas, however, fences should be moved several times a day, depending upon how large the area is and how many horses are inside the pasture. Another disadvantage is the potential for a wild animal to accidentally run through the fence and break it. (It doesn't matter if Old Dollar and pals are used to the fence, a bull moose isn't.) To prepare for this possibility, you might want to hobble your horses inside the fence.

When using an electric fence, again, choose an area with good forage. Scattered brush is acceptable, but make sure that grass is the dominant vegetation type. Hobble your horses after you have led them inside the fence, then step outside and turn it on. If you have worked with them, the horses should stay in the fence without any problems. Remember to move the fence often.

Electric fences can be used in conjunction with hobbling as well by placing the herd boss inside the fence and leaving the other hobbled horses outside.

It's common to let a herd of horses loose at camp without restraint while keeping the herd boss restrained. Loose herding is a great way to minimize impact, because grazing and trampling are spread over a large area. With this technique, it is possible to camp in an area and move on with little indication that the area has ever been used. The disadvantage to loose herding, however, is that horses are not as easily controlled. Thus there is more chance that your horse may run off in the night.

A compromise option is to leave most horses loose while keeping a saddle horse restrained by a more secure method, thereby leaving you an animal to ride if all of the other horses decide to head back to the trailhead. You can use this horse to wrangle the others with in the morning.

Where grazing is not allowed, some other means of confinement is needed. The two acceptable options are to use existing corrals and hitchracks, or to use highlines or picket lines. These techniques can also be used once grazing is completed, in places where picketing is not allowed, or in situations where loose herding and hobbling seem undesirable at night. (Tying the horses to trees overnight is not acceptable.) Both methods result in substantial impact; the key is to confine that impact to as small an area as possible.

Existing corrals and hitchracks that have little or no vegetation have already been trampled so much that it is unlikely that further use will harm these areas. When using a hitchrack, space your horses far enough apart so they won't get tangled. Before turning horses loose together in a corral, make sure they are acquainted with one another. Unless you plan to feed horses on the site, remember that corrals and hitchracks are only temporary holding areas. They are good places to tie up your horses when you are working with them, such as saddling and loading. Use only existing structures; don't build them.

Tying horses to a highline or picket line is an effective method of keeping animals near camp, but it can be highly destructive. Rangers in Yellowstone National Park, for instance, discourage the use of highlines, recommending instead picketing, loose herding, hobbling, or using electric fences. On the other hand, some places encourage the use of highlines. As with picketing, this technique is a compromise between security and impact concerns. Impact potential is high, but impact can be minimized with care.

When seeking a place to put a highline, look for places that have already been used for highlines. In previously unused areas, look for a durable, nonvegetated area between

NOLS

Riding and packing with horses in the backcountry can be an enjoyable and memorable recreational experience.

trees. Concentrate your use in one site. The highline area should be far enough away from trees that trampling of roots or damage to trunks will not occur. When tying the ends of the highline to trees, it is best to use cinches or double-wrapped rope to avoid cutting into bark and girdling the trees. Some manufacturers supply "tree-saver" straps that serve the same purpose. Nervous horses that paw the ground should always be hobbled.

Whatever method you choose, take steps to minimize impact as much as possible. Upon leaving a camp, try to repair some of the evidence of your stay. A little work at the end of a trip can ensure that those who follow will never know you were there.

Keep in Mind
Riding a horse in the backcountry can be one of the most enjoyable recreational experiences today. From the back of a

horse, you can enjoy the scenery, watch for wildlife, and enjoy the companionship of a hard-working animal.

But horsepacking can and does carry a necessary burden of responsibility. When using a horse, you have assumed a commitment for the safety of yourself, your horse, and the environment. Without special care, pack stock can quickly damage fragile wildlands.

As with any recreational activity, what you do affects those who follow; however, using minimum-impact techniques will help reduce impact to the backcountry and preserve it for the enjoyment of those who follow.

Reduction is essential to the horsepacker who wants to ensure light-on-the-land techniques. This should be done in a number of ways:

1. Reduce the number of animals.
2. Reduce the duration of stay.
3. Reduce the level of confinement in camp.

Plan Ahead and Prepare
- Know your animal, its habits and tendencies.
- Work with your horse before the trip.
- Take along the right, lightweight gear.
- Familiarize yourself with your destination. Call land managers and obtain maps.

On-Trail and Off-Trail Travel
- Keep horses single file on trails.
- Spread out when riding off-trail to avoid creating a path.
- Choose durable rest areas well off the trail when you stop.
- Tie horses to trees for short periods only.

Choosing the Best Campsite
- Concentrate use in impacted areas.
- Look for sites well off the trail away from other parties.

- In pristine areas, spread out use, and take extra care to avoid impact.
- The availability of feed and the potential for minimizing impact should determine campsite selection.

Extended Camping
- Move camp periodically, even if it's just across a large meadow.

In Camp
- Give horses supplemental feed in feed bags or on a tarp or poncho.
- Water horses in durable sites where trampling damage can be kept to a minimum.

Grazing and Restraint
- There are four options for handling stock when grazing: hobbling, picketing, electric fencing, and loose herding.
- Hobbling can be one of the best ways to minimize impact.
- Picketing is a good way to keep a single dominant horse near camp, thus controlling other horses. Be sure to move pickets often.
- An electric fence can work well for minimizing impact, but it should cover a large area and be moved often.
- Loose herding spreads out use and thus is an excellent minimum-impact tool.
- Existing hitchracks and corrals should be used for confining horses for short periods of time only. Never build them.
- Highlines and picket lines are also good methods of confining horses but should be done only on durable surfaces, preferably for a short time, when other options aren't readily available or practical.

A Final Thought

Perhaps the only thing harder than writing a book about ethics is reading one. Wildland users value independence; we don't want anyone suggesting what we should do or how we should act. After all, no one dictated our forebears' behavior in wilderness. Today when we go to the wilds, we seek some of that same freedom from society's rules.

Yet how easily we forget that only a short while ago wilderness had an entirely different meaning. There were few of us then, and wilderness was something that stood in the way. We fought it, cursed it, and feared it. Not until recently, with civilization crowding what little wildland remained, did we decide that wilderness has deep-rooted values. As John Muir observed, "Thousands of tired, nerve shaken, over-civilized people are beginning to find out that going to the mountains is going home: that wildness is a necessity . . ."

Today, more than 105 million acres of wildlands in the United States are protected by the National Wilderness Preservation System established by the Wilderness Act in 1964. These lands are threatened, however, by thousands and thousands of "overcivilized people," so much so, in fact, that whereas we once measured human success by the ability to survive wilderness, we must now ask whether wilderness can survive humankind. Indeed, human activity has become such a pervasive influence on earth's ecological framework— humans having altered more than one-third of earth's terrestrial landscape—that soon it may no longer be possible to separate people and nature. Pockets of wilderness may survive, but marking boundaries and setting aside remote areas is not enough. Nor are regulations imposed by land managers once damage has been done. Those of us who use this land must take responsibility for its health. Aldo Leopold said it best: "Health is the capacity of the land for self-renewal. Conservation is our effort to understand and preserve this capacity."

Exactly how healthy our wildlands will be in the future depends on our behavior every time we hike a trail or canoe a river. If our use is wise, the land won't suffer unduly from our presence, and others may have a similarly unique experience. In this respect, a wildland ethic may be the most important item we carry into the backcountry, as well as the most important lesson we take back home to our everyday lives.

A wildland ethic should not be a burden. It should come naturally, just as concern and responsibility for those you love comes as you mature. But first you must learn about your wildlands and how to travel softly on them. Get experience, preferably from knowledgeable companions or a school offering a qualified outdoor program. It's not enough to read a book. Too often, inexperienced visitors find they have to compromise certain practices because a mountain or a river handed them something they were not expecting. Building a fire at timberline because you forgot to bring repair parts for your stove or losing your food to a bear because you couldn't tie the correct knot to hang it in a tree isn't practicing a wildland ethic. Plan ahead. Be organized. Anticipate difficulties so that you will not have to compromise truly responsible behavior.

Everyone using the backcountry for wildland recreation, be it climbing, fishing, hunting, backpacking, horsepacking, or river running, should have one objective in common: participation governed by self-conscious restraint. Accepting and following an ethic with the integrity of the land foremost in mind, we transcend the obvious goal of climbing a summit, catching a five-pound trout, or hiking twenty miles to camp beside an alpine lake. The original goal soon fades, and we are left with the deep satisfaction that comes with rekindling a profound respect for the land. A sign at the entrance to Tanzania's Manyara National Park, close to where human beings first stood on the edge of the world and saw wilderness everywhere, best sums it up:

> *Let no one say and say it to your shame*
> *that all was beauty here until you came.*

Further Reading

The scientific foundation needed to mitigate environmental impact on wildlands is woefully inadequate. Part of the problem is that the science of wilderness management is relatively new and loosely structured; after all, recreational impact itself has only recently become widespread. But some of the fault must fall on all of us in the environmental community. In our struggle to increase the amount of designated backcountry land, we've been blind to the problems caused by our own use. By ignoring these problems and not encouraging the research that will guide future use, we've been shortsighted. We may secure more wildlands only to discover that they've lost much of their value because of poor stewardship.

With the call for more knowledge about recreational impact, the following list of publications provides source material for readers desiring more information regarding recommendations found in the text.

1. The Case for Minimum Impact

Cole, D. N. 1989. Low-impact recreational practices for wilderness and backcountry. General Technical Report, INT-265. USDA Forest Service, Intermountain Research Station, Ogden, UT. 51 pages.

Cordell, H. K., ed. 1999. *Outdoor Recreation in American Life: A National Assessment of Supply and Demand Trends*. Sagamore Publishing, Champaign, IL. 246 pages.

Frome, M. 1985. *Issues in Wilderness Management*. Westview Press, Boulder, CO. 252 pages.

Hammitt, W. E., and Cole, D. N. 1998. *Wildland Recreation: Ecology and Management*. 2nd edition. John Wiley and Sons, New York. 361 pages.

Hart, J. 1998. *Walking Softly in the Wilderness.* Sierra Club Books, San Francisco, CA. 478 pages.

Hendee, J. C., and Dawson, C. P. 2002. *Wilderness Management.* 3rd ed. Fulcrum Publishing, Golden, CO. 640 pages.

Kloepger, D., and Marsh, S., eds. 1992. *Keeping It Wild: A Citizen's Guide to Wilderness Management.* The Wilderness Society, Washington, DC. 70 pages.

Marion, J. L., Roggenbuck, J. W., and Manning, R. E. 1993. Problems and practices in backcountry recreation management: a survey of National Park Service managers. Natural Resources Report NPS/NRVT/NRR-93/12. USDI, National Park Service, Natural Resources Publication Office, Denver, CO. 48 pages.

Nash, R. F. 1982. *Wilderness and the American Mind.* Yale University Press, New Haven, CT. 425 pages.

2. Backcountry Travel

Anderson, D. W., and Keith, J. O. 1980. The human influence on seabird nesting success: conservation implications. *Biological Conservation.* 18:65–80.

Boyle, S. A., and Samson, F. B. 1985. Effects of nonconsumptive recreation on wildlife: a review. *Wildlife Society Bulletin.* 13:110–116.

Cassirer, E. F., Freddy, D. J., and Ables, E. D. 1992. Elk responses to disturbance by cross-country skiers in Yellowstone National Park. *Wildlife Society Bulletin.* 20:375–381.

Cole, D. N. 1993. Trampling effects on mountain vegetation in Washington, Colorado, New Hampshire, and North Carolina. USDA Forest Service Research Paper INT-464. Intermountain Research Station, Ogden, UT. 56 pages.

Cole, D. N. 1995. Experimental trampling of vegetation. II. Predictors of resistance and resilience. *Journal of Applied Ecology.* 32:215–224.

Hall, C. N., and Kuss, F. R. 1989. Vegetation alteration along trails in Shenandoah National Park, Virginia. *Biological Conservation.* 48:211–227.

Harlow, W. M. 1977. Stop walking away the wilderness. *Backpacker*. 5(4):33–36.

Knight, R. L., and Gutzwiller, K. J., eds. 1995. *Wildlife and Recreationists: Coexistence through Management and Research*. Island Press, Washington, DC. 373 pages.

Kuss, F. R. 1983. Hiking boot impacts on woodland trails. *Journal of Soil and Water Conservation*. 38:119–121.

Leung, Y., and Marion, J. L. 1996. Trail degradation as influenced by environmental factors: a state-of-knowledge review. *Journal of Soil and Water Conservation*. 51:130–136.

Leung, Y., and Marion, J. L. 2000. Recreation impacts and management: a state-of-knowledge review. In Cole, D. N., McCool, S. F., Borrie, W. T., and O'Loughlin, J., comp. Wilderness science in a time of change conference. Vol. 5: Wilderness ecosystems, threats, and management. USDA Forest Service General Technical Report RMRS-P-15-VOL-5. Ogden, UT. Pages 23–48.

MacArthur, R. A., Geist, V., and Johnston, R. H. 1982. Cardiac and behavioral responses of mountain sheep to human disturbance. *Journal of Wildlife Management*. 46:351–358.

Manning, R. E. 1999. *Studies in Outdoor Recreation: Search and Research for Satisfaction*. 2nd ed. Oregon State University Press, Corvallis, OR. 374 pages.

Stankey, G. H. 1980. A comparison of carrying capacity perceptions among visitors to two wildernesses. USDA Forest Service Research Paper INT-242. Intermountain Forest and Range Experiment Station, Ogden, UT. 34 pages.

Turner, T. 1986. Rush hour in the national forests. *Sierra*. 71(3):26–28.

van Wagtendonk, J. W. 1981. The effect of use limits on backcountry visitation trends in Yosemite National Park. *Leisure Sciences*. 4:311–323.

Washburne, R. F., and Cole, D. N. 1983. Problems and practices in wilderness management: a survey of managers. USDA Forest Service Research Paper INT-304. Intermountain Forest and Range Experiment Station, Ogden, UT. 56 pages.

3. Selecting and Using a Campsite

Brown, P. J., and Schomaker, J. H. 1974. Final report on criteria for potential wilderness campsites. USDA Forest Service Intermountain Forest and Range Experiment Station, Missoula, MT. 50 pages.

Cole, D. N. 1982. Controlling the spread of campsites at popular wilderness destinations. *Journal of Soil and Water Conservation.* 37:291–295.

Cole, D. N. 1987. Research on soil and vegetation in wilderness: a state-of-knowledge review. Proceedings— National Wilderness Research Conference: Issues, State of Knowledge, Future Directions. USDA Forest Service General Technical Report INT-220. Intermountain Research Station, Ogden, UT. Pages 135–177.

Cole, D. N. 1993. Campsites in three western wildernesses: proliferation and changes in condition over 12 to 16 years. USDA Forest Service Research Paper INT-463. Intermountain Research Station, Ogden, UT. 15 pages.

Cole, D. N. 1995. Disturbance of natural vegetation by camping: experimental applications of low-level stress. *Environmental Management.* 19:405–416.

Cole, D. N., and Benedict, J. 1983. Wilderness campsite selection—what should users be told? *Park Science.* 3(4): 5–7.

Cole, D. N., and Fichtler, R. K. 1983. Campsite impact and frequency of use in three western wilderness areas. *Environmental Management.* 7:275–288.

Cole, D. N., Watson, A. E., Hall, T. E., and Spildie, D. R. 1997. High-use destinations in wilderness: social and biophysical impacts, visitor responses, and management options. USDA Forest Service Research Paper INT-RP-496, Ogden, UT. 30 pages.

Frissell, S. S., and Duncan, D. P. 1965. Campsite preference and deterioration in the Quetico-Superior canoe country. *Journal of Forestry.* 63:256–260.

McEwen, D., and Cole, D. N. 1997. Campsite impact in wilderness areas. *Parks and Recreation.* 32(2):24–32.

Marion, J. L., and Cole, D. N. 1996. Spatial and temporal variation in soil and vegetation impacts on campsites. *Ecological Applications.* 6:520–530.

Merriam, L. C., Jr., and Smith, C. K. 1974. Visitor impact on newly developed camp sites in the Boundary Waters Canoe Area. *Journal of Forestry.* 72:627–630.

4. Fires and Stoves

Bratton, S. P., Stromberg, L. L., and Harmon, M. E. 1982. Firewood-gathering impacts in backcountry campsites in Great Smoky Mountains National Park. *Environmental Management.* 6:63–71.

Cole, D. N., and Dalle-Molle, J. 1982. Managing campfire impacts in the backcountry. USDA Forest Service General Technical Report INT-135. Intermountain Forest and Range Experiment Station, Ogden, UT. 16 pages.

Fenn, D. B., Gogue, G. J., and Burge, R. E. 1976. Effects of campfires on soil properties. National Park Service Ecological Service Bulletin No. 5. Washington, DC. 16 pages.

Hall, T. E., and Farrell, T. A. 2001. Fuelwood depletion at wilderness campsites: extent and potential ecological significance. *Environmental Conservation.* 28:241–247.

Harmon, M. E., Franklin, J. F., Swanson, F. J., et. al. 1986. Ecology of coarse woody debris in temperate ecosystems. *Advances in Ecological Research.* 15:133–302.

Harvey, H. T., Hartesveldt, R. J., and Stanley, J. T. 1972. Wilderness Impact Study Report. Sierra Club Outing Committee, Palo Alto, CA. 87 pages.

Maser, C., Tarrant, R. F., Trappe, J. M., and Franklin, J. F. 1988. From the forest to the sea: a story of fallen trees. USDA Forest Service General Technical Report PNW-229. Pacific Northwest Research Station, Portland, OR. 153 pages.

Stanley, J. T., Harvey, H. T., and Hartesveldt, R. J., eds. 1979. A report on the wilderness impact study: the effects of human recreational activities on wilderness ecosystems with special emphasis on Sierra Club wilderness outings in the Sierra Nevada. Sierra Club Outing Committee, Palo Alto, CA. 290 pages.

5. Sanitation and Waste Disposal

Brickler, S., Tunnicliff, B., and Utter, J. 1983. Use and quality of wildland water: the case of the Colorado River corridor in the Grand Canyon. *Western Wildlands*. 9:20–25.

Cilimburg, A., Monz, C. A., and Kehoe, S. K. 2000. Wildland recreation and human waste: a review of problems, practices and concerns. *Environmental Management*. 25:587–598.

Holmes, D. O. 1979. Experiments on the effects of human urine and trampling on subalpine plants. Proceedings— Recreational Impact on Wildlands. Report No. R-6-001-1979. USDA Forest Service, Pacific Northwest Region, Portland, OR. Pages 79–88.

Meyer, K. 1989. *How to Shit in the Woods*. Ten Speed Press, Berkeley, CA. 77 pages.

Silsbee, D. G., and Larson, G. L. 1982. Bacterial water quality: springs and streams in the Great Smoky Mountains National Park. *Environmental Management*. 6:353–359.

Silverman, G., and Erman, D. C. 1979. Alpine lakes in Kings Canyon National Park, California: baseline conditions and possible effects of visitor use. *Journal of Environmental Management*. 8:73–87.

Stuart, D. G., Bissonette, G. K., Goodrich, T. D., and Walter, W. G. 1971. Effects of multiple use on water quality on high-mountain watersheds: biological investigations of mountain streams. *Applied Microbiology*. 22:1048–1054.

Suk, T. J., Riggs, J. L., and Nelson, B. C. 1986. Water contamination with Giardia in backcountry areas. Proceedings— National Wilderness Research Conference: Current Research. USDA Forest Service General Technical Report INT-212. Intermountain Research Station, Ogden, UT. Pages 237–244.

Suk, T. J., Sorenson, S. K., and Dileanis, P. D. 1987. The relation between human presence and occurrence of Giardia cysts in streams in the Sierra Nevada, California. *Journal of Freshwater Ecology*. 4:71–75.

Taylor, T. P., and Erman, D. C. 1979. The response of benthic plants to past levels of human use in high mountain lakes in Kings Canyon National Park, California, USA. *Journal of Environmental Management.* 9:271–278.

Temple, K. L., Camper, A. K., and Lucas, R. C. 1982. Potential health hazard from human waste in wilderness. *Journal of Soil and Water Conservation.* 37:357–359.

6. Deserts

Belnap, J., Harper, K. T., and Warren, S. D. 1994. Surface disturbance of cryptobiotic soil crusts: nitrogenase activity, chlorophyll content, and chlorophyll degradation. *Arid Soil Research and Rehabilitation.* 8:1–8.

Belnap, J. 1998. Choosing indicators of natural resource condition: a case study in Arches National Park, Utah, USA. *Environmental Management.* 22:635–642.

Cole, D. N. 1985. Ecological impacts on backcountry campsites in Grand Canyon National Park, Arizona, USA. *Journal of Environmental Management.* 10(5):651–659.

Dunne, J. 1989. Cryptogamic soil crusts in arid ecosystems. *Rangelands.* 11(4):180–182.

Johnson, R. R., and Carothers, S. W. 1982. Riparian habitat and recreation. Eisenhower Consortium Bulletin 12. Rocky Mountain Forest and Range Experiment Station, Fort Collins, CO. 31 pages.

Wallace, A., Romney, E. M., and Hunter, R. B. 1980. The challenge of a desert: revegetation of disturbed desert lands. *Great Basin Naturalist Memoirs.* 4:216–225.

Whitson, P. D. 1974. The impact of human use upon the Chisos Basin and adjacent lands. National Park Service Scientific Monograph Series 4, Washington, DC. 92 pages.

7. Rivers and Lakes

Carothers, S. W., Johnson, R. A., and Dolan, R. 1984. Recreational impacts on Colorado River beaches in Glen Canyon, Arizona. *Environmental Management.* 8:353–360.

Cole, D. N. 2000. Managing campsite impacts on wild rivers: are there lessons for wilderness managers? *International Journal of Wilderness.* 6(3):12–16.

Frissell, S. S., Jr., and Duncan, D. P. 1965. Campsite preferences and deterioration in the Quetico-Superior canoe country. *Journal of Forestry.* 63:256–260.

Hartmann, L. A., Freilich, H. R., and Cordell, H. K. 1989. Trends and current status of participation in outdoor recreation. In Outdoor Recreation Benchmark 1988, Watson, A. H., ed. USDA Forest Service General Technical Report SE-52. Southeastern Forest Experiment Station, Asheville, NC. Pages 147–165.

Knudsen, A. B., Johnson, B. B., Johnson, K., and Henderson, N. R. A. 1977. Bacterial analysis of portable toilet effluent at selected beaches along the Colorado River, Grand Canyon National Park, Arizona. Proceedings—River Recreation Management and Research Symposium. USDA Forest Service General Technical Report NC-28. North Central Forest Experiment Station, St. Paul, MN. Pages 290–295.

Manning, R. E. 1979. Impacts of recreation on riparian soils and vegetation. *Water Resources Bulletin.* 15:30–43.

Williams, J., and Monz, C. A. 1994. Fragile rivers: current knowledge regarding minimum impact use and identification of significant research gaps. Proceedings—The Third North American Interdisciplinary Wilderness Conference, Ogden, UT, Nov. 1993. Vause, L. M., ed. University of Nevada Press, Reno.

Zaslowsky, D. 1986. *These American Lands.* Henry Holt and Company, Inc., New York. 404 pages.

8. Coasts

Anderson, D. W., Mendoza, J. E., and Keith, J. O. 1976. Seabirds in the Gulf of California: a vulnerable international resource. *Natural Resources Journal.* 16:483–505.

Baker, C. S., Herman, L. M., Bays, B. G., and Bauer, G. B. 1983. The impact of vessel traffic on the behavior of humpback whales. Proceedings—First Glacier Bay Science Symposium. USDI, Science Publications Office, Atlanta, GA. Page 54.

Carlson, L. H., and Godfrey, P. J. 1989. Human impact management in a coastal recreation and natural area. *Biological Conservation*. 49:141–156.

Gajda, A. M. T., Brown, J., Peregoodoff, G., and Bartier P. 2000. Managing coastal recreation impacts and visitor experience using GIS. In Cole, D. N., McCool, S. F., Borrie, W. T., and O'Loughlin, J., comp. Wilderness science in a time of change conference. Vol. 5: Wilderness ecosystems, threats, and management. USDA Forest Service General Technical Report RMRS-P-15-VOL-5. Ogden, UT. Pages 115–123.

Ghazanshahi, J., Huchel, T. D., and Devinny, J. S. 1983. Alteration of southern California rocky shore ecosystems by public recreational use. *Journal of Environmental Management*. 16:379–394.

Godfrey, P. J., and Godfrey, M. M. 1980. Ecological effects of off-road vehicles on Cape Cod. *Oceanus*. 23(4):56–66.

Kay, A. M., and Liddle, M. J. 1989. Impact of human trampling in different zones of a coral reef flat. *Environmental Management*. 4:509–520.

Kury, C. R., and Gochfeld, M. 1975. Human interference and gull predation in cormorant colonies. *Biological Conservation*. 8:23–34.

Marion, J. L., and Rogers, C. S. 1994. The applicability of terrestrial visitor impact management strategies to the protection of coral reefs. *Ocean & Coastal Management*. 22:153–163.

Povey, A., and Keough, M. J. 1991. Effects of trampling on plant and animal populations on rocky shores. *Oikos*. 61:355–368.

Robertson, R. J., and Flood, N. J. 1980. Effects of recreational use of shorelines on breeding bird populations. *Canadian Field-Naturalist*. 94:131–138.

9. Alpine and Arctic Tundra

Arno, S. F. 1984. *Timberline*. The Mountaineers, Seattle, WA. 304 pages.

Billings, W. D. 1987. Constraints to plant growth, reproduction and establishment in arctic environments. *Arctic and Alpine Research.* 19:357–365.

Cole, D. N., and Monz, C. A. 2002. Trampling disturbance of high-elevation vegetation, Wind River Mountains, Wyoming, U.S.A. *Arctic, Antarctic, and Alpine Research.* 34: Pages 365–376.

Cooper, D. J. 1985. The Arrigetch Peaks region of the central Brooks Range, Alaska: ecosystems and human use. Proceedings—National Wilderness Research Conference: Current Research. USDA Forest Service General Technical Report INT-212. Intermountain Research Station, Ogden, UT. Pages 94–99.

Edwards, O. M. 1979. Vegetation disturbance by natural factors and visitor impact in the alpine zone of Mt. Rainier National Park: implications for management. Proceedings—Recreation Impact on Wildlands Conference. USDA Forest Service, Pacific Northwest Region, Portland, OR. R6-001-1979. Pages 101–108.

Forbes, B. C. 1992. Tundra disturbance studies. II. Plant growth forms of human-disturbed ground in the Canadian far north. *Musk-ox.* 39:164–173.

Grabherr, G. 1982. The impact of trampling by tourists on a high altitudinal grassland in the Tyrolean Alps, Austria. *Vegetatio.* 48:209–217.

Hartley, E. 2000. Thirty-year Monitoring of Subalpine meadow vegetation following a 1967 trampling experiment at Logan Pass, Glacier National Park, Montana. In Cole, D. N., McCool, S. F., Borrie, W. T., and O'Loughlin, J., comp. Wilderness science in a time of change conference. Vol. 5: Wilderness ecosystems, threats, and management. USDA Forest Service General Technical Report RMRS-P-15-VOL-5. Ogden, UT. Pages 124–132.

McCloskey, J. M., and Spalding, H. 1988. A reconnaissance-level inventory of world wilderness areas. In Martin, V., ed. *For the Conservation of the Earth.* Fulcrum Inc., Golden, CO. Pages 18–30.

Monz, C. A. 2002. The response of two arctic tundra plant communities to human trampling disturbance. *Journal of Environmental Management.* 64:207–217.

Price, M. F. 1985. Impacts of recreational activities on alpine vegetation in western North America. *Mountain Research and Development.* 5(3):263–277.

Willard, B. E., and Marr, J. W. 1971. Recovery of alpine tundra under protection after damage by human activities in the Rocky Mountains of Colorado. *Biological Conservation.* 3:181–190.

Zwinger, A. H., and Willard, B. E. 1972. *Land above the Trees: A Guide to American Alpine Tundra.* Harper and Row, New York. 489 pages.

10. Snow and Ice

Ells, M. D. 1997. Impact of human waste disposal on surface water runoff, the Muir Snowfield, Mount Rainier. *Journal of Environmental Health.* 59:6–12.

Ferguson, M. A., and Keith, L. B. 1982. Influence of Nordic skiing on distribution of moose and elk in Elk Island National Park, Alberta. *Canadian Field-Naturalist.* 96:69–78.

Hammitt, W. E., McDonald, C. D., and Hughes, J. L. 1985. Experience level and participation motives of winter wilderness users. Proceedings—National Wilderness Research Conference: Current Research. USDA Forest Service General Technical Report INT-212. Intermountain Research Station, Ogden, UT. Pages 269–277.

11. Bear Country

Cushing, B. 1983. Responses of polar bears to human menstrual odors. Proceedings—Fifth International Conference on Bear Research and Management, International Association for Bear Research and Management. Pages 275–280.

Herrero, S. 1985. *Bear Attacks: Their Causes and Avoidance.* Nick Lyons Books/Winchester Press, Piscataway, NJ. 287 pages.

Schneider, B. 1977. *Where the Grizzly Walks*. Mountain Press Publishing Co., Missoula, MT. 191 pages.

Servheen, C. 1985. Biological requirements of a wilderness species. Proceedings—National Wilderness Research Conference: Current Research. USDA Forest Service General Technical Report INT-212. Intermountain Research Station, Ogden, UT. Pages 173–175.

12. Horsepacking

Aaland, D. 1993. *Treading Lightly with Pack Animals*. Mountain Press Publishing Co., Missoula, MT. 140 pages.

Cole, D. N., and Spildie, D. R. 1998. Hiker, horse, and llama trampling on native vegetation in Montana. *Journal of Environmental Management*. 53:61–71.

DeLuca, T. H., Peterson, W. A. IV, Freimund, W. A., and Cole, D. N. 1998. Influence of llamas, horses and hikers on soil erosion from established recreation trails in western Montana. *Environmental Management*. 22:255–262.

Harmon, D., and Rubin, A. S. 1992. *Llamas on the Trail*. Mountain Press Publishing Co., Missoula, MT. 170 pages.

Hill, O. C. 1989. *Packing and Outfitting Field Manual*. University of Wyoming, Laramie, WY. 110 pages.

McClaran, M. P. 2000. Improving livestock management in wilderness. In Cole, D. N. McCool, S. F., Borrie, W. T., and O'Loughlin, J., comp. Wilderness science in a time of change conference. Vol. 5: Wilderness ecosystems, threats, and management. USDA Forest Service General Technical Report RMRS-P-15-VOL-5. Ogden, UT. Pages 49–63.

McClaran, M. P. and Cole, D. N. 1993. Packstock in wilderness: use, impacts, monitoring, and management. USDA Forest Service General Technical Report INT-301. Intermountain Research Station, Ogden, UT. 33 pages.

Mionczynski, J. 1992. *The Pack Goat*. Pruett Publishing Co., Boulder, CO. 147 pages.

Spildie, D. R., Cole, D. N., and Walker, S. C. 2000. Effectiveness of a confinement strategy in reducing pack stock impacts at campsites in the Selway-Bitterroot Wilderness, Idaho. In Cole, D. N., McCool, S. F., Borrie, W. T., and O'Loughlin, J., comp. Wilderness science in a time of change conference. Vol. 5: Wilderness ecosystems, threats, and management. USDA Forest Service General Technical Report RMRS-P-15-VOL-5. Ogden, UT. Pages 199–208.

Stoner, M. 1993. Techniques and equipment for wilderness travel with stock. Report 9323-2839-MTDC. United States Forest Service, Technology and Development Program, Missoula, MT. 60 pages.

Index